Every Manager's Guide
to Information Technology

EVERY MANAGER'S GUIDE TO INFORMATION TECHNOLOGY

A GLOSSARY OF KEY TERMS AND CONCEPTS FOR TODAY'S BUSINESS LEADER

PETER G.W. KEEN

HARVARD BUSINESS SCHOOL PRESS
BOSTON, MASSACHUSETTS

The paper used in this publication meets the requirements of the American
National Standard for Permanence of Paper for Printed Library Materials
Z39.49-1984.

Library of Congress Cataloging-in-Publication Data

Keen, Peter G.W.
    Every manager's guide to information technology: a glossary of key terms
    and concepts for today's business leader/Peter G.W. Keen.
    p. cm.
    Includes index.
    ISBN 0-87584-309-3 (pb; alk. paper):
    1. Information technology—Dictionaries.   I. Title.
    HC79.I55K44   1991
    004'.024658—dc20   91-21250   CIP

Cover and text design: Eleanor Bradshaw

Contents

PREFACE

When you travel to a strange city or country, it is helpful to have a guide. Surely your effectiveness will be diminished if you have to rely on sign language or are simply handed a dictionary and told, "This has everything you need to speak Transerbosanskrit and talk to the natives. Off you go."

Every Manager's Guide to Information Technology is my effort to be, literally, a guide. I wrote this book because I need it in my work as an educator and consultant and I couldn't find its equivalent anywhere, and I hear constantly from teachers, managers, journalists, and legislators about the need for a shared language in dealing with technical specialists and vendors of IT products and in assessing business opportunities to exploit IT—telecommunications plus computers plus multimedia information.

The problem is not just technobabble, the notorious jargon of IT, but the lack of a core set of concepts and terms. The problem with preparing a comprehensive, dictionary-like glossary is that straight definitions of the thousands of IT terms—with dozens of new ones emerging virtually every month— do not differentiate the key terms managers need to know, and why, nor do they relate the technical issues to business and to business management.

In this Glossary I have highlighted what I see as the core terms and concepts in IT. Most of my own work as a professor, consultant, writer, management educator, researcher, and manager of the world's smallest multinational involves translating business and technical issues for business managers and technical professionals. The Glossary summarizes the language I have found essential to that translation.

A fashionable view among some consultants and teachers is that managers do not need such a language, that it is the responsibility of IT professionals to explain IT in business terms, and that IT jargon is irrelevant and superfluous. Yes...but. There can be no question that business must drive technology and that IT experts must not hide behind the obscurantism of technospeak. But business managers do need to understand some aspects of the technology. Throughout this Glossary, the reader will find discussions of deceptively simple nonjargon terms such as "integration," "standards," "testing," and "networks," terms that can enable the computer-fluent manager who understands their implications to make a direct, positive, and powerful contribution to the business-IT dialogue and planning process. Knowledge here is empowerment, and lack of knowledge is to be a tourist adrift in a foreign land. Almost every week I see examples of skilled business managers being victims of IT; they accept recommendations of well-intentioned technical specialists without knowing what questions to ask or what trade-offs to make concerning choices of technology that later turn out to have major business impacts. They didn't know what they didn't know.

I hope and believe this Glossary can reduce that risk. Rather than merely give definitions, I provide business examples, business inter-pretations, and assessments of the business implications of technical terms. I have aimed at being simple, but not simplistic; selective, but not misrepresentative; and rigorous, but not pedantic or overdetailed. I have also tried to make the Glossary interesting and readable: a frequent blockage to business managers' understanding of IT is the way in which an exciting and fascinating field is made to appear boring, obscure, and intimidating.

How little, rather than how much, do business managers need to know about IT? I hope this Glossary is just about enough.

Peter G.W. Keen
May 1991

ACKNOWLEDGMENTS

Writing a book is the easy part. Publishing a book is much more complex. The first draft is an intensely personal statement that writers, in my view and in my own experience, find hard to let go of. The distancing and reshaping of the statement into the work that readers hold in their hands demand a collaborative effort. You need an editor equally committed to helping you make your statement and to getting the work to readers effectively and efficiently. This book is my third with Carol Franco as my editor, and I am thankful for her commitment, judgment, and support (and tolerance). She may not have improved my writing, but I have certainly improved my books with her help.

You need a developmental editor who tailors the original statement, as needed and often necessarily ruthlessly, without losing its personality and voice. This is my second book of which John Simon has been the re-shaper. The result is a different and much better text. He has played a creative, not just blue-pencil role in its structure, content, and format.

My wife, Lynda, has spent about as much time on this book as I have. Without her, it would have been later and less focused. It would also have been a very different book; I wrote it, but together we shaped it.

Every Manager's Guide to Information Technology

Introduction

The story of information technology is a story of nonstop change. The rate of change, in business and organizations as well as in the technology itself, is obvious. The on-line society—in the form of automated teller machines, computerized reservation systems, computer-integrated manufacturing, and point-of-sale transaction processing—is emerging rapidly; the "networked" organization is moving from cliché to possibility to practicality, with telecommunications playing an increasing role in coordinating geographically dispersed operations. There is today little that we might predict about IT that would seem implausible.

Internationally, as well, information technology is a force for change—social, political, and economic. The world bore witness, via telecommunications, to major events as they happened: first in Tiannamen Square, then in Wenceslas Square, and, more recently, in the Persian Gulf. A new international economy is rising on the shoulders of information technology; daily, more than $1 trillion a year is moved by electronic funds transfers and more than $300 billion by foreign exchange transactions. By contrast, the total world trade in physical goods is about $4 trillion—less than a week's worth of international funds transfers.

IT is a business force now. It amounts to one-half of U.S. firms' annual capital expenditures and increasingly affects how firms organize, do business, and compete. Business managers who choose not to reckon with it do so at their and their firms' peril.

The Vocabulary of Change

IT, like many other disciplines, has spawned a bewildering array of terms and concepts. This book presents these from the perspective not of how much, but of how little, business managers need to know about the technology to manage IT as effectively as they manage money, people, and materials. Because delegating most aspects of IT planning to technical specialists and consultants was the norm in almost all companies for nearly thirty years, information technology has not been as natural a part of business managers' everyday language as financial terms and concepts.

Often, business managers must sign off on IT recommendations that they cannot fully assess. They are told that "electronic data interchange" is a growing competitive necessity, but that there are many different "standards," that the firm needs an "architecture," and that "local area networks" are a core requirement for a particular department, but there are problems of "incompatibility" between the departmental "LAN" and the corporate "data-base management systems." How can they sift through the necessary jargon and zero in on the business implications and options?

Telling business managers, as many have, that they must become "computer literate" is a little like telling them that they must become automobile literate in order to operate a car. One does not need to comprehend the mechanics of the transmission system, engine, and catalytic converter to drive well or do transportation planning effectively. A core vocabulary of terms and an insight into the relationships and trade-offs among a few of them will suffice. Literacy focuses on *what*, fluency on *why*. This book aims at helping the IT manager become *fluent* in IT. Thus it answers not only the question "What is a local area network?", but also "Why is the choice of a local area network important to our business strategy and performance?" and "What issues do we as business managers need to know about to make sure that the planning and decision making for local area networks meet business, economic, and organizational as well as technical needs?"

Responsibility for answering such questions has traditionally been delegated to people well equipped to reply to the first, but with little knowledge to bring to bear on the second or third questions. Delegations is not a strategy. Too often it amounts to abdication— of opportunity, control, and responsibility. Delegation was a reasonably safe approach as long as IT was peripheral to business and organizational growth and health. Today IT affects virtually every area of business, hence virtually every manager.

Change can be a threat or an opportunity. It can be anticipated or reacted to. IT and change are now synonymous. In many industries taking charge of change is impossible without taking charge of IT. Vocabulary is the starting point for doing so. In accounting and finance, for example, business managers must be familiar with a few fundamental terms— e.g., overhead, depreciation, marginal costing. Lack of awareness of, say, the difference between marginal cost, average cost, and allocated cost can easily lead to incorrect business judgments. But business managers need only understand what depreciation is, not the detailed formulas for calculating it.

We take this level of knowledge of the basics of accounting for granted in business managers. In its absence, planning and decision making are almost sure to miss their targets. In Central Europe and the USSR, because highly placed managers and government officials are unfamiliar with these basics, they frequently do miss them. U.S. executives, consultants, and educators doing business there are frustrated with blockages to dialogue, misallocation of resources, and breakdowns in planning because of the lack of knowledge about the basics of business.

Examples of how blindness to the basics of IT can impede dialogue, resource allocation, and planning abound. Consider the concept of "integration," which is fundamental to the effective deployment of IT. Today Information Services managers are wrestling with immense operational problems created by "incompatibility" and trying to develop coherent "architectures." Integration refers to the linking of individual IT components and services for the purpose of sharing software, communications, and data resources. Incompatibility is diametrically opposed to integration; architecture is the blueprint for achieving it.

Many business managers, seeing such terms as excuses for creating a new IT bureaucracy, are likely to focus on decisions about individual components and applications—for instance, review their department's needs for personal computers—on the basis of cost and features. This is common sense. Only later, when the departmental system will not link directly to the firm's major processing systems and the data resources they create, do they discover the hidden costs of incompatibility and lack of attention to architecture. Extra software and equipment are added to enable the personal computers to access the corporate information resources only to find that cross-links among business services and transactions are blocked because each had a separate technology base. Often it is close to impossible to remove the blockages without redesigning and rebuilding all of the systems.

This manager's guide illustrates how and why these problems occur, as well as identifies the major components of the IT resource. It highlights the issues business managers face in making trade-offs between meeting immediate needs through individual applications and anticipating future needs that can be met only with an integrated architecture.

It is as easy for contemporary U.S. business managers to view terms such as architecture, integration, and compatibility as technical abstractions as it is for Soviet managers to see depreciation and marginal costs in this light. Therefore many firms are spending enormous sums to rationalize a muddle of multitechnology, multivendor systems that cannot share information and communications. A whole new industry of "systems integrators" has developed in the past few years to address the frequency, cost, and blockages to business progress of systems disintegration.

It is not unusual for a large firm to have as many as one hundred incompatible major systems and forty incompatible communications networks. When business functions and departments were largely independent of one another, this was not a major problem; a firm's financial system did not need to cross-link to distribution and manufacturing, for example, nor did its European purchasing system need to share information with its U.S. production system. Once a firm establishes these connections—and if the technology is there, some firm is bound to do so—its competitors are at a disadvantage for as long as they fail to follow; and the longer they wait, the more difficult it becomes to follow.

It is not unusual for business managers unfamiliar with the exigencies of integration to be told that particular standards, vendors, and software can end their problems immediately and forever, only to discover that the tidy consultants' or vendors' presentations contained more theory than reality and obscured many important practicalities. It is here that the jargon of IT can be overwhelming. The need to cross-link business services often gets sidetracked from business issues to discussions of UNIX, OSI, X.25, SNA, X.400, RS-232, SQL, and other bits of the IT alphabet soup. Each term has a precise and important meaning; each is necessary to technical planners and implementers. Indeed, it is as unfair to criticize IT professionals for indulging in technospeak as it would be to fault bankers for moving from simple business discussions about investing spare funds in short-term, interest-yielding instruments to estoterica about Fannie Maes, Ginnie Maes, T-bonds, CDs, and so forth.

IT professionals, like any professionals, need a specialized language in which to hammer out details. That many such encounters leave business managers perplexed is because the discussions are not dialogues. The manager has no context for the technical terms and, alas, too many IT experts are ignorant of business issues and language, particularly about costs and organizational factors that affect the outcome and value of IT investments. Often they are very assertive about issues that in practice are controversial and uncertain. As a result, business managers may feel that a technical recommendation or prediction is "the" truth, that implementation is easy and automatic, and that the proposed investment is the only way to go. They listen to a monologue instead of being part of a dialogue.

No one today can be thoroughly familiar with IT terminology; the field has become so broad that even experts are often unfamiliar with terms outside their area of specialization. The worlds of computers and telecommunications, in particular, evolved along separate technical and organizational paths with the result that few specialists in either area are conversant in both.

Effective dialogue—between business managers and technical specialists, as well as between technical specialists in different areas—rests on a shared understanding of a relatively small number of key concepts and terms, as was pointed out earlier in the examples of accounting and finance. Without this rapport, advisers and clients, managers and IT experts, can work together only on a "trust me—take it or leave it" basis. The stakes have become too great and the pace of change too fast for such delegation to be a viable choice for managers for whom IT has become a part of their core business. Hence I have prepared this management guide—not a comprehensive, but rather a very selective "glossary" of a small fraction of key IT terms and concepts, which not only provides definitions, but helps managers to understand which of the terms are germane to computer fluency and how they relate to major IT choices and options from a business perspective.

The Glossary is deliberately selective. The problem with a comprehensive glossary of IT terms is that it does not help managers sort out which terms are key to their activities and which terms they can ignore. Here is an example: A glossary of 5,000 terms assigns equal importance to "V.21" and "X.400." From a technical perspective, V.21 (which refers to how computer equipment links to a telephone network) is more important than X.400 in many companies' IT planning. But from a business perspective, X.400 is a major development that opens up many business and organizational opportunities. A basic aim in evolving this Glossary is to highlight the terms that, if understood, can assist managers in recognizing business opportunities, making sound decisions, and establishing effective dialogues with IT planners and managers.

That makes this a book about business, not about technology.

Evolution of the IT Management Process

An underlying theme in the Glossary is the management process of IT in organizations. Understanding this may help explain some of the problems that business managers see in how IT costs are handled, for example, or how new information systems are developed, how changes are made to existing systems, and how new technologies are introduced.

Many of the planning and accounting procedures, attitudes, and relationships in place today in organizations reflect a thirty-year tradition of delegation in information systems management and of handling IT costs and planning as budgeted overhead. The management process has not kept pace with technology—its uses and pervasive impact and the policy decisions needed to make it effective. Therefore professionals and business managers face one another across a gulf and frequently experience mutual frustration trying to bridge it. A shared language helps, but more important is a shared understanding of the decision issues that underlie the language. To merely define integration and architecture, for example, affords little insight into what these elements imply for the planning process or business managers' contributions to it.

In retrospect, we can identify four fairly distinct eras in the evolution of IT in organizations:

- Data processing (DP) (1960s)

- Management information systems (MIS) (1970s)

- Information innovation and support (IIS) (1980s)

- Business integration and restructuring (BIR) (1990s)

Much of the present IS management practice was developed in the MIS era and is now being adapted to meet the stresses and challenges of the IIS era A relatively small number of firms are positioning to using IT as a business resource that can help them rethink and restructure their organizations and business operations; a personal estimate is that perhaps 20 percent of the *Fortune* 1000 are at that stage or almost there, with a slightly higher fraction for smaller firms that are less constrained by old management practices for managing IT because they began their use of IT with the personal computer not with data processing units.

The Data Processing Era

Computers first became economically attractive for large and medium-sized companies in the 1960s. At that time they were very expensive and very limited in application. As every computer was incompatible with every other one until well into the 1970s, the word "incompatible," being assumed, was rarely used.

Developments in computer use were hardware-driven, relying on improvements in equipment costs, capacity, and speeds; and applications had to be built from scratch, as the third-party supplier of packaged software was not yet in existence. Telecommunications was confined almost entirely to telephones until the 1970s, when "voice" phone lines began to be used to provide access to computers from remote terminals. The transmission techniques for early data communications were slow and expensive. Because telecommunications was entirely regulated and choices of technology restricted, companies had no need to develop in-house any beyond operational telecommunications skills. Telecommunications was an operational backwater; the action was in data processing.

The economics of computer use during this era pushed firms toward automating large-scale clerical activities—hence the label "data processing." (Staff at a number of U.S. government agencies sill routinely speak of ADP—automated data processing.) Payroll and accounting applications were natural targets of opportunity. Given that a computer that cost, say, $5 million could be justified only in terms of displacing large numbers of fairly low-level administrative or clerical staff, the natural starting points for data processing were clerical activities that involved repetitive, high-volume transactions based on applying automatic rules, calculations, and procedures.

Automating these functions turned out to be much harder than anticipated. Computer programmers with little if any business experience, interest, and aptitude had to wrestle with a new and complex technology, developing methods as they went along. The field was young, as were the people in it. Their value to the business—their analytic skills and infatuation with the technology proved also to be their limitation. They tended to be intellectually and titillatingly unable to put themselves in the shoes of "users," who were frequently afraid of losing their jobs or influence because of computers and of looking foolish because they did not understand them, or were annoyed at the condescension of programmers. The research literature in the IT field in the early 1970s frequently identified "resistance to change" as a major explanation of why systems that worked technically so often failed organizationally; there is plenty of evidence that much of this resistance was to computer people, not to computers.

DP developed as a specialized staff function isolated from the business. The isolation was both psychological and physical. Many companies placed their DP units in new buildings designed to house large computers; those were frequently many miles away from any of the business operations; DP people rarely saw their users.

Even when they did, what was mainly on their minds were today's DP problems. Taming the technology, developing systematic project management methods, absorbing a flood of new programming languages, and managing operations consumed DP's resources and attention. The head of DP was almost invariably someone who had come up through the ranks in the programming field. He—there were a few shes at the top in DP, even though this was the first major business field in which skilled women were welcomed because of the often desperate shortage of capable staff—operated a factory dominated by systems development, central operations, and increasing investments in "maintenance," a somewhat misleading term for the work needed to keep existing systems functioning effectively and efficiently. When the tax law changed, the payroll system had to be modified; the firm could not say, "But we like the old tax laws; we'll keep them." Few if any experts in DP ever anticipated that maintaining old systems would consume more effort and resources than building new ones. In the 1990s, those old systems are a concrete block on the feet of Information Services desperately trying to meet the business demand for new ones.

Except when a major systems development project affected their sphere of authority and responsibility, business managers has little interaction with DP. Generally, the people who worked with DP in specifying systems were lower-level supervisors. Frequently, busy business units were reluctant to release their best staff to work with DP, and the people assigned were those who were expendable. This hardly improved the quality of design.

Because fully half of application development projects badly overran their budgets, failed to perform satisfactorily relative to expectations and needs, or were abandoned before completion, business executives tended to view DP as a problem rather than as an opportunity. Furthermore, since it was both a new field and peripheral to the mainstream of business, it was not an attractive career option for most business managers. It had been neither part of their college and management education nor part of their personal development.

It was a frustrating situation for the best data processing professionals, who very often had outstanding analytic skill and were ferociously hard-working and self-motivated and honestly committed to delivering first-rate systems. Their explanations of the frequent foulups in software development highlighted users' not knowing what they wanted, constantly changing specifications, and not being willing to commit their time, knowledge, and prestige to the project. It was in this period that computer people began to be seen as "different" from business people.

They also were seen as expensive. Business managers came to view DP as an escalating cost, to be carefully controlled. This was achieved principally by allocating costs on a formula basis to the departments that used the DP organization's services. Allocations were generally charged out so that DP expenses were fully recovered. Some firms ignored allocations, instead absorbing the costs centrally, with systems development projects paid for by the targeted business unit.

For many business units, "chargeouts" were frustrating; unit managers could not control IT costs, did not see much value from IT, and felt that IT professionals were not only too highly paid, but also far too ready to move on to the next lucrative job in the programmers' boom market of the 1960s through the mid-1980s. IT allocations were like a corporate property tax on business units.

The technology of the 1960s and 1970s was characterized by large economies of scale. A reliable rule of thumb was that a computer twice the cost of the one in place would provide four times the power. This led naturally to an emphasis on centralization and to planning being driven by hardware decisions. Because it was expensive, hardware was treated as a capital item; the less-expensive staff resource became an annual expense.

Because development was not viewed as a capital item, few firms, even today, have any idea how much has been spent to create the software systems they have in use. Since the accounting system expensed salaries for development and maintenance staff as well as operators, firms did not track the relationships between these cost elements over the life cycle of a major system. Today, firms are discovering that most of the costs of IT are hidden. For instance, the costs of support and education for a personal computer are far higher than the purchase price, and the cost of developing a system is often a fraction of the cost of operations and maintenance.

Spending on computers was largely determined by an annual budgeting process. Next year's budget was set by aggregating business units' requests for new systems, comparing the firm's own expenditures as a percentage of sales with that of comparable companies, and capping the budget increase at X percentage. In a good year, X went up; in a tough year, it was held constant or cut. The systems development and operations plan was fine-tuned within these parameters.

The heritage of the DP era remains a strong force in many firms. The following are among its remnants.

Naive chargeout mechanisms that block investment in longer-term infrastructures. If costs must be fully recovered and there is no central funding, the initial users must bear the total investment. Today, users can often find less expensive alternatives in increasingly cost-effective personal computers, departmental communications, and off-the-shelf software. Cost allocations and recovery schemes are two of the major impediments to integration and architecture, since they discourage long-term investments in infrastructures that must be paid for by the early users.

A broad gulf between senior business managers and IT managers. Typical forty-year-old or fifty-year-old executives—for whom computers were not part of their education, not part of their move up the management ladder, and, in their new-found senior status, not a necessary personal tool—are ill-prepared to play an active role in major IT policymaking and planning. "I am proud to say that I have worked in every single area of the company except computers and that will be true when I retire," boasted the CEO of one *Fortune* 100 company publicly. More common is the manager who says, "I am too old to learn about computers."

A firm grounding in computing. Computing provided the main body of experience, expertise, and authority for information technology; telecommunications played almost no role. But this scheme is shifting rapidly. Yesterday's add-on is today's infrastructure. Telecommunications today is the highway system over which the traffic of an increasingly distributed resource travels.

A continuing bottleneck in software development and the burden of old systems. DP lost much credibility because it so rarely delivered on its promises. One leading authority, Frederick Brooks, who led the development of one of the largest civilian software development efforts ever when he worked at IBM, coined the term "the mythical man-month" to describe programmers' estimates of how long a project would take; typically, the figure was well over 100 percent too optimistic. Successes in systems development were overshadowed by delays, cost overruns, and bugs for most of the 1960s and 1070s. Large-scale software engineering is a difficult craft even today; the experiences of those years persist, but not for lack of effort, skill, or commitment on the part of development staff. The process is inherently complex and software productivity continues to lag behind other areas of information technology.

The Management Information Systems Era

With most basic clerical and accounting processes automated by the mid-1970s, the focus of attention in Information Systems shifted to designing and building reporting systems to meet managers' information needs. These efforts were largely flawed for two reasons: limitations in the technology and the mistaken equating of "information" with "data." The technology of this period was still that of the data processing era—large, expensive, inflexible computers that generated enormous volumes of data, typically historical, highly detailed, and accounting-based. The rationale of MIS was to organize and present this data to managers, assuming almost by definition that the more data they had the better.

In practice, the data met few managers' needs; for example, because reports generally lagged events by several months, they were of little value for competitive analysis or for spotting trends and problems early enough to react constructively. Moreover, accounting data yielded only limited information for management decision making. Its primary value was for planning and administration. Changes in the technology gradually opened up new opportunities for turning data into information and tailoring systems to meet managers' real needs.

One important new tool for doing this was the computer terminal, which for the first time permitted flexible, occasional, and ad hoc access to central information stores and to "time-shared" processing on large computers. Time-sharing was an innovation that allowed a large computer to process many tasks (or jobs) simultaneously by giving each a small slice of time and going from one to the other very quickly. The result was that many people doing different work at the same time could be "logged on" to the computer. Given the economies of scale of computing, this encouraged the growth of time-sharing "bureaus" that could offer services individual firms could not afford. Time-sharing is still the base for today's airline reservation systems and automated teller machines.

Another useful tool that emerged in the 1970s and helped speed up the development of systems was packaged software, sets of programs written by third-party developers. Most of these addressed needs that did not require company-specific software development: report generation, financial modeling, and general ledger accounting, for example. The combination of time-sharing and flexible packages and modeling languages stimulated rapid innovation in what would be termed "decision support systems" and "end-user computing," a process that personal computers accelerated, principally because the operating costs of time-sharing were high and those of personal computers low.

Almost all of this innovation occurred outside the central MIS units, especially in finance or marketing departments, where small teams of business-oriented planners picked up the new tools and applied them imaginatively. Management Information Systems groups, like the mainstream technology they controlled, remained monolithic. The problem of balancing control and innovation led to continued crisis for MIS throughout the mid-1970s. When computers first came into companies, few if any control groups managed them, and the most effective units were those that encouraged experimentation. But to the extent that they managed to "sell" the wonders of the new technology, they created a demand that they could not reliably meet. Experimentation too easily became chaos. Costs escalated. Planning procedures were informal, at best. Software development was an ad hoc process, with undocumented, untested, and unmaintainable "spaghetti" code a frequent result. Testing and maintenance were neglected as the overcommitted DP group tried to catch up with a systems development backlog that averaged from three to five years of resources.

The MIS era saw efforts to introduce discipline and professionalism and to control MIS costs and resources more sensibly. Too often, control created bureaucracy. With MIS wrestling with major changes in technology and continued and growing problems in software development and project management, and senior executives interested in getting costs under control, the Information Systems function found itself increasingly on the defensive. MIS staff rarely understood the business, and few business executives understood MIS.

Most stereotypes of computers and computer people date from this period. Remember "Do not fold, spindle, or mutilate"? Were you among those who received bills for $00.00 and subsequent notice that legal proceedings would be initiated if payment were not forthcoming? Maybe you were one of the managers who received massive computer printouts of monthly reports. At the very least, you were probably informed in response to an inquiry that "the computer made a mistake."

Given that during this era most innovation occurred outside the MIS area, it is not surprising that MIS professionals became frequent resisters of change. The widespread early opposition of most, though by no means all, central MIS units to the introduction of personal computers in the early 1980s was a case in point. MIS staff wrote off the new "micros" as machines for amateurs, viewing themselves as the "experts" on matters relating to computers; they worried, justifiably, about problems of testing, documentation, and security.

If this summary of the MIS era sounds negative, it is because little of a positive nature occurred during the period. The field of MIS ossified at a time when that of office technology, end-user computing, and decision support systems began to flourish. MIS became stuck in an organizational, technical, and attitudinal rut; it failed to build a constituency (few business units viewed the traditional MIS group as more than a necessary part of operations overhead); it had no strong management sponsor.

That said, although the problems it faced were sufficiently complex that many persist today—notably large-scale software development and maintenance of old systems—MIS was not without substantive achievements. Its principal technical development was the shift from transaction processing to data base management. In the DP era, the main challenge was computer programming, which relied on quirky minds to develop immensely detailed and precise instructions to carry out even simple transactions or generate reports. Data files—weekly payroll records, customer history files, or purchase orders— were organized for processing efficiency, and data were frequently duplicated. A bank, for example, would store customer names and addresses in each pertinent master file for a business application; checking account, mortgages, savings, and so forth. Changes of address had to be entered in each file.

Inconsistency, redundancy, and duplication of data became commonplace and contributed to the bureaucratization of the MIS function, adding considerably to the data administration burden of user departments and customers.

The MIS era saw the creation of the concept of data-base management systems (DBMS), an innovation that has evolved slowly but consistently over the past fifteen years. With a DBMS, data are organized in much the same way as books are in a library. Information such as a name and address is stored in only one place, on a computer tape or disk. The DBMS software includes the equivalent of the library's index of authors and subjects. A transaction processing or report program request the customer record, which the DBMS retrieves, just as a borrower uses the library's card catalogue to locate the shelf and unique reference number for a book. Any number of programs thus access the same data items, instead of storing them many times over in separate files. When information such as a customer's address is changed, the DBMS locates the relevant item and updates it. The DBMS will also check for errors and handle such aspects of security as providing access to information only to authorized users.

A library catalogues books by title and subject, but not by chapter or diagram. The evolution of DBMS has been toward the most detailed level of indexing—the equivalent of indexing a book by phrase or word. Initially, data were organized in records; a customer master record might contain many data items, including last name, first name, middle initial, social security number, home phone number, and so on. Early DBMS accessed information at the record level. "Relational data-base management systems" access it at the item level and allow very complex searches through data bases in order to answer such questions as, "Show me all the customers in ZIP code 20007 with outstanding balances of more than $500 who own their own homes."

Data-base management software incurs substantial processing

overhead and, for most of the MIS era, was too expensive for many applications and completely impractical for major transaction processing systems. But in shifting the focus from programming to data and data management, the genesis of data-base management systems marked a turning point in the role of Information Systems organizations. More and more, IS is becoming a cornerstone in the balanced coordination of key, shared, corporate infrastructures and decentralized use of IT. With this shift, the old centralized data centers housing mainframe computers have been turned into information libraries.

The Information Innovation and Support (IIS) Era

The history of IT in large organizations has been a pendulum, swinging between extremes of innovation and discipline and thus of emphasis on decentralization and centralization. As the pendulum swung back from the freewheeling days of early DP, it met the discipline of MIS.

Indeed, the MIS era marked the extreme of centralization in computing. And there the pendulum hung, through the ossification of traditional MIS, before swinging back toward innovation and a deliberate lack of overrestrictive discipline, first in the early use of personal computers and then in the transformation of both the technology and its uses that subsequently made innovation the norm. We call this position of the pendulum the era of Information Innovation and Support.

The swing away from overdiscipline, which began in the early 1980s, was fueled primarily by changes in the technology, most obviously office technology and personal computers. These created an entirely new market for IT. The term "information technology" replaced "computers," "information systems," and "data processing," as telecommunications became the access vehicle for computing services, data-base management systems were opened to proliferating personal computers, and low-cost, do-it-yourself software flooded the market.

Office technology was the first step in the organizational perestroika of IT. Business units purchased word processors from a wide range of vendors; personal computers appeared on the desks of many professionals and some executives; and minicomputers and microcomputers introduced an alternative for departmental computers beyond what came to be called "mainframes." Not a real option in the 1970s at a price of $5 million, departmental machines were practical at $100,000 in the 1980s and $25,000 or even less in the early 1990s. Time-sharing on mainframes was expensive in the 1970s and early 1980s, costing anywhere from $20 to $200 an hour.

The microprocessor-based personal computer, as much an economic as technical innovation, boasted an operating cost of pennies per hour. With this technology, the analyst who wanted to run *what if?* analyses of budgets for ten hours a week no longer had to justify more than $20,000 annually for time-sharing. Initially, MIS units mostly either ignored, blocked, or tried to control such innovations. The skill base of MIS rested on traditional programming languages, transaction processing systems, and formal project management methods, all of which remained important and will remain important in the future. Inertia in MIS actually stimulated the shift toward business unit autonomy, reinforced and even hastened by the personal computer. Business managers now had choices outside the old MIS monopoly, and they exercised those choices.

They also looked at computers through a new lens. Just about every major application in the DP and MIS era looked inward, at the company's own operations. The IIS era looked outward and searched for sources of competitive advantage from IT. Indeed, IT-and- competitive-advantage became almost one word in the early 1980s. Consultants and academics chased after examples of firms that had gained—or that seemed to have gained—a sustained edge over their competitors by using IT.

Some of these examples were overhyped; the advantage turned out to be transitory, or where it was real the firm got in trouble because of something totally unrelated to IT, thus showing that IT could never substitute for business vision, organization, and management. That said, the new focus on competition, business, service, and customers helped transform the mindset of IS, and its vocabulary.

Part of sweeping away the cobwebs came from telecommunications. By the mid-1980s, the technology of telecommunications had begun a transformation that continues to be even more radical and spectacular than that of computers. The telephone lines of the 1970s, designed to carry voice traffic, were slow, unreliable, and very expensive for moving computer data. Local area networks, fiber optics, satellite technology, and a wide range of new equipment that exploited microprocessors increased the speeds and reduced the costs of telecommunications by factors of hundreds in the 1980s, a pace that looks slow compared with what is happening in the 1990s.

Deregulation of long-distance services in the United States stimulated fierce competition, imaginative new products, technological innovation, and new sources of supply. Large firms were no longer confined to POTS—plain old telephone systems— but could design their own telecommunications infrastructures that could deliver a wide range of electronic services In addition, local area networks, which enabled personal computers to be linked at low cost across short distances within a building, provided a base for explosive growth in departmental computing and data management facilities. The resulting IT resources were more powerful, yet far more cost-effective and easy to manage, than the DP shops of the 1970s.

Together, telecommunications and personal computers liberated the use of IT in organizations. Without efficient and low-cost data communications, decentralized departmental computers could not share information among themselves. For information to be shared across business units and functions, computers had to be centralized. The growing availability of telecommunications led to what is termed "distributed" systems, a combination of workstations linked to mid-sized departmental computers or central mainframes or both. Computers could now be located anywhere and linked among companies as well as departments.

The combination of frustration with the rigidities of traditional centralized MIS, the ready availability of personal computers and packaged software, and local and wide area telecommunications that enabled them to be connected with one another and with larger computers, shifted the focus of IT from automation to innovation. This search for innovation has been explicit and encompasses all areas of

IT. The role of MIS shifted to trying to position IT as a new source of competitive opportunity and advantage, in part by supporting the now-institutionalized, distributed, and effectively autonomous users of personal computers.

Individuals exploited electronic spreadsheets, laptop computers, word processing, and desktop publishing; groups and departments exploited electronic mail, local area networks, and shared data resources; business units transformed customer service. Companies embraced IT as a way to just-in-time everything—on-line ordering, computer-integrated manufacturing, JIT inventory; the list grows.

The mentality of the new Information Services units that grew out of MIS shifted from control to coordination and support. The Information Services' view of distributed systems built from the mainframe outward, first linking personal computers to central services and information stores, and then redesigning transaction processing, communications, and data-base management systems to exploit the strengths of each element. The implementation of these strategies is variously termed the "client/server model" and "cooperative processing."

The old MIS career path of programmer to project leader to manager was complemented, and in many instances supplanted, by a career path emphasizing a level of business understanding that was virtually nonexistent before. Growth of knowledge and bridging the attitude gaps between business and IS professionals became priorities. Management "awareness education programs for senior executives," "help" desks for personal computer users, and IS steering committees were typical initiatives. IS and business units encouraged the development of a new form of hybrid staff, skilled in business and knowledgeable about IT or vice versa. Leading IS managers, increasingly called chief information officers or CIOs opened the MIS fortress and emphasized business support as the priority for IS. (The renaming of DP to MIS and MIS to IS was not a gimmick but a real effort to signal shifts in the role of the IT unit.)

Today innovation is everywhere, much of it uncoordinated. Many "islands" of IT have been created, partly because business units were able to go their own way rather than depend on MIS, but mostly because the entire technology base, large scale and small scale, has been dominated by "incompatibility." Every major vendor's equipment—hardware, software, telecommunications, and data management—has been "proprietary." IBM and Apple Macintosh personal computers, Ethernet and Token Ring local area networks, Digital Equipment Corporation's VMS and IBM's MVS operating systems, and most telecommunications networks were incompatible with one another. There are technical, marketing, and political explanations for this, but the reasons matter far less than the impacts.

The most farsighted IS managers viewed with growing concern the fragmentation and incompatibilities among systems across the firm. As long as units remained self-contained islands, lack of integration was not a problem and could even be an advantage in that it enabled them to choose technology solely on the basis of what best suited their needs. But more and more elements of business were becoming interdependent: departments needed to share information with other locations and functional areas, and business units increasingly needed to combine data to create new products and services. Meanwhile, the cost of supporting multiple networks and software escalated. The absurdities of incompatibility meant that personal computers within a department could not even read files that had been word processed on another personal computer, use the same printer, or share a local area network, and efforts to link major transaction processes and rationalize telecommunications turned these simple local systems into organizationwide messes.

Whereas business units naturally placed priority on autonomy, quick installation, and low-cost operation, IS focused on the need for integration, immediately or later. "Architecture" became a key term in IS but not in most users' vocabularies. The dismal track record of old-line MIS led may users to view "architecture," "integration," and "standards" as rear guard efforts to reestablish control. The major barrier to central coordination was the very same tool that provided the most cost-effective IT base for user departments—the local area network. This area of IT innovation was easily the one most beset by incompatibility. The calculus of the 1980s favored innovation at the risk of loss of discipline. But local innovation turned out to have its own costs and limitations, and the pendulum began to swing back again toward the end of the 1980s.

The Business Integration and Restructuring (BIR) Era

Today the pendulum is swinging back toward an innovative discipline that balances central coordination of key IT infrastructures and the use of IT within these infrastructures with decentralized autonomy in decisions about applications. As the costs of incompatibility became clearer to IT users and providers, the telecommunications community mounted a major effort to create "open systems." Committees defined "standards" that would enable equipment manufactured by different vendors to be connected in order to provide various types of services. The user community played an increasingly active role in the standard-setting process, creating a number of de facto standards by its choices of vendors and systems. The IBM personal computer is a ready example of how a "proprietary" system, by virtue of gaining substantial market share, became an effectively "open" one. The success of the IBM PC led other vendors to create "IBM-compatible" products. They could not legally fully replicate IBM's hardware, so they built products that ran under the IBM PC's software operating system, called MS.DOS. Today, DOS machines are everywhere; it was users who created this situation through their own purchasing decisions.

Standards, integration, and open systems moved to the top of the IS management agenda in the early 1990s. A new industry of systems "integrators" had emerged that grew at a rate of 20 percent a year, largely because there was so much systems disintegration to repair. Standard-setting committees focused on ending the Tower of Babel of incompatibility. For the first time, vendors anticipated the need to make sure their systems were compatible instead of trying to lock customers in through proprietary systems in the way that IBM and Apple had.

The ACE (Advanced Computing Initiative) group was established by twenty-one firms in April 1991 to create a standard for "multivendor networked computing." Whether this effort will be a success is debatable, since defining standards takes many years, and implementing standards in real products can take longer—if, in fact, the standard can be defined in the first place, the implementations can be made complete and consistent, and innovations in the technology do not make the standard obsolete, and if vendors do not add their own special "nonstandard" features. That said, the ACE initiative marks the style of the 1990s; it could never have occurred in the 1970s, when proprietary systems were the norm. Open systems are now the enthusiastic or reluctant target of every major vendor and user.

The question today is how to achieve them. Because the standard-setting process cannot keep up with the pace of change in technology, there are many gaps in standards, and much more controversy about the implementation potential of many that have been defined.

But the major policy issues in IT, from a business perspective, concern investments in infrastructures. The Information Innovation and Support era largely emphasized applications—new purchasing systems, local area networks, workstations for computer-aided design and manufacturing, funds transfer networks, and so forth. Formal policies on standards, because they were viewed as bureaucratic, tended to be avoided.

Today, with business integration driving technology integration, standards are seen as essential. Insurance firms increasingly rely on shared cross-product customer data resources for cross-selling and targeted marketing; more and more customers and suppliers are linking their IT bases through electronic data interchange to eliminate paper documents such as purchase orders and invoice; transnational firms are connecting previously separate international systems in order to coordinated operations across twenty-four time zones.

Leading IT thinkers and practitioners have recently begun to question the ethos of automation that underlies the origins of IT. Terms such as "business process reengineering" and "informate instead of automate" have become the new watchwords of the IT profession in what is becoming part of a general rethinking of principles of organizational design in large enterprises; "teams," "communication," the "networked organization," and "collaboration" are replacing traditional emphasis on planning, hierarchy, decision making, and control. The restructuring of organizational processes and structures is emerging as a business priority, with IT as a powerful potential contributor, especially through telecommunications, which removes barriers of location and time on coordination, service, and collaboration.

The view of IT as a major enabler of new forms of organization includes new interorganizational relationships and processes, and a mechanism for streamlining and eliminating work rather than automating it. Electronic data interchange is but one of many contemporary examples. As more and more large firms insist that suppliers link to them electronically or lose their supplier relationship, EDI becomes less an option and more an imperative.

In the retailing industry, electronic data interchange and "quick response" systems have enabled a few firms to reduce to a few days their logistics cycle for ordering and stocking; the gap between the leaders and the laggards is so pronounced that it is no surprise that most experts expect that fully half of today's retailers will be out of business in 2001. The "very quick" response firms in the fabric industry take ten days from getting an order from a store to delivering the goods, while the "average" response firms take 125 days. The same patterns and impacts are apparent in the logistical systems of insurance firms in terms of lead times to issue a policy, and manufacturers in "time to market." IT is now about how firms carry out their business and how they relate to suppliers and customers. We have come a long way from the DP era.

In this context, business managers cannot delegate IT as they once did. They can still delegate the technical work, but not the planning that drives it. Because defining, funding, and implementing infrastructures, architecture, and integration involve long lead times and crossing functional boundaries, they demand top-level policy attention and careful definition of business and organizational priorities to guide the choice of standards and pace and degree of integration.

This is the context in which we ask the question, "How little do managers need to know about IT to play an effective role in planning its use?" The answer is, "Enough to help move the firm forward to the era of business integration and restructuring."

The Glossary

How much of the vocabulary of IT is enough for business managers who need to restructure and integrate their firms? Earlier we referred to the vocabulary of change—the terms and concepts with which a manager must be familiar to understand and meaningfully discuss change.

We have made the case that to a great extent change in IT has become change in business. It is this circumstance that has occasioned the call for "hybrid" managers: IT managers fluent in the vocabulary of change for business and business managers fluent in the vocabulary of change for IT. The latter are the audience for this book.

A guiding principle in the drafting of *Every Manager's Guide to Information Technology* was the recognition that a business manager is, after all, a business manager; hence the Glossary presents a highly selected vocabulary, a supplement to the manager's primary vocabulary. Furthermore, its terms and concepts are less defined than discussed. There are other sources to which the business manager can turn for precise technical definitions of any of the thousands of IT terms.

The Glossary emphasizes the technical context and the business relevance of the terms and concepts it presents. Thus the many permutations of networks—local area, wide area, value-added—are discussed in one place in terms of their individual characteristics, relationships to one another, and business relevance, both individually and in the aggregate. The business manager who has read the Glossary entry under "networks" will have the advantage of a general understanding when consulting reference sources for more comprehensive definitions of particular types of networks.

The Glossary carries the emphasis on context further by providing for each entry a list of other entries that are relevant to a broader basis for understanding the term or concept. Hence the Glossary entry for "networks" includes cross-references to terms that relate to the technical basis of networks (e.g., "bandwidth," "mobile communications," "protocol," "satellites," and "transmission"), terms that relate to the context of providers (e.g., Regional Bell Operating Companies), and terms that relate to the business relevance of or functional responsibility for networks (e.g., "architecture," "chief information officer").

Business managers are busy people. The author knows this first-hand, having consulted with many of them. Hence the design and organization of the Glossary. It is slim enough to fit into a briefcase without displacing a manager's "work" and large enough to occupy a place on the shelf among other "computer" books without getting lost. It can be browsed through on a plane or a train, or while waiting for either. But most usefully, it is a convenient dispenser of context at a moment's notice. "Oh, by the way, there'll be some people from corporate IS at the meeting this afternoon to talk about a way our field people can get into our network through them." "Hmm, not through 'them,'" you think, nodding to your colleague and reaching for your Glossary. "They must have a scheme for using mobile communications. I seem to recall that there's a security issue associated with that."

The cross-referencing in the Glossary is so extensive that if you were to look up all the related terms for each entry you consulted, and the related terms for each of those terms, you would soon have finished the book. But, of course, you needn't. A quick glance at most terms, in some cases even at the associated marginalia, will be sufficient to make a determination whether to read further. The entry on "networks" and enough related terms to provide a context for attending the meeting mentioned above could probably be read in five minutes. The purpose, after all, is to prepare for meaningful discussion, not to go head to head with IS people on technical issues.

On the shop floor today, there is a call for "renaissance engineers"; at the level of running the business, we must have "renaissance managers." *Every Manager's Guide to Information Technology* is offered as one of the textbooks in "Renaissance Management 101."

Glossary

Acronym   See Jargon and Acronyms

AI   See Artificial Intelligence

American National Standards Institute (ANSI)   Founded in 1918, the American National Standards Institute (ANSI) is the central organization for the development of standards not only for information technology but for American industry in general. The 1,300 member organization also represents the United States in international standard-setting activities.

The standard-setting process relies on organizations such as ANSI to provide a forum for vendors and users to reach agreement—on standards for telecommunications, programming languages, equipment interfaces, and new technologies. An ANSI standard carries weight in the marketplace, though like all IT standards, it has no legal status.

See also: Standards

Setting an IT standard is rather like making an international trade treaty. The relevant parties have to get together, make deals, and reach an agreement. ANSI provides a forum for this, rather like GATT, NATO, or the United Nations.

American Standard Code for Information Interchange (ASCII)   The American Standard Code for Information Interchange, or ASCII, is one of the earliest and simplest standards for representing computer data. It is a code for representing numbers and alphabetic characters in digital form—that is, as ones and zeros. IBM rejected

ASCII and had already created its own coding scheme, EBCDIC, as the basis for its computers. ASCII, extended ASCII, and EBCDIC are the three coding schemes most widely used to represent data.

An "ASCII file" is a data file that any program should be able to read. In practice, many packages have unique conventions for representing information, particularly details of formatting. Data stored in a way that facilitates computation, compact storage, and rapid retrieval (accounting and marketing data, for example) typically does not employ ASCII coding.

Most acronyms in the IT field are pronounced as written. ASCII is "askeey."

See also: Standards

Analog   See Digital

ANSI   See American National Standards Institute

Apple   See Personal Computer

Application Software and Application Development   An application is a business or organizational use of a computer. Application development is the design and implementation of the software facilities to support such use, and is the core activity of Information Systems units. Payroll, invoicing, and salary administration are applications. Each may involve the development of many individual software programs.

Application software is distinguished from systems software, which supports the effective and efficient operation of application programs and is usually provided by the manufacturer of the computer hardware on which the applications run. Operating systems, for example, control the processing steps of an application program, handle errors, and manage links to printers, data base files, and switching among the many programs that constitute the application.

On a mainframe computer, the operating system may have to manage literally hundreds of application programs simultaneously. It may access stored libraries of routines, support dozens of different programming languages, and act as a traffic cop as several programs try to access the same data base. Communications control programs handle the flow of messages into and from the applications. File utility, security, and data-base management software similarly manage the access and updating of data bases, ensure error-checking and security, and perform other "housekeeping" functions.

Traditionally, applications have been developed by systems analysts and application programmers who translate the target business requirements into a technical system design and then write, test, and install the needed programs using programming languages such as COBOL (for business applications) and FORTRAN or C (for more technical and scientific applications). An invoicing system, for example, may entail the development of programs to sort and validate input data, update master records, create invoices, and generate management reports.

Application development dominates the planning of Information Systems (IS) departments and their relationships with the users of the systems they develop. IS departments' business plans are built largely around their application portfolios, with each major development project involving a business unit client that is generally desperately concerned with cost, delay, and quality, especially when the new system is a key element in marketing, product innovation, or customer service. Major development projects are likely to take at least two years to complete. An experienced application programmer will typically produce around 30 lines of computer program code per day. A new billing system for a large firm can easily amount to a million lines of program code—20,000 pages of computer printout requiring about 140 person years to complete.

Successful application development relies on (1) the ability to build relationships and dialogue with business units, (2) systems development and project management skills, and (3) client support, especially education. IS units are trying to broaden the skill base of their development staffs, a base that traditionally has been focused on technical rather than business and organizational skills. For many years, IS units built application systems in isolation from the people who understood the context of the work, information, and procedures.

Backlogs of systems development projects still average 2–3 years of staff resources in large companies, just as they did in the 1980s, 1970s, and 1960s.

The difficulties of just making the technology work drove out organizational considerations and dialogue with users. As IS groups have come to recognize that such dialogue is essential, the profile of the application development professional has broadened beyond traditional programming skills.

For four decades, the IS field has been preoccupied with speeding up application development and improving the quality of application software. Although some progress has been made, application development causes the same problems and bottlenecks it did in the 1970s and 1980s. Capers Jones, one of the leading authorities on application development, estimates that more than 60 percent of large systems projects have "significant cost and schedule overruns" and 75 percent of completed systems exhibit operational difficulties, high maintenance costs, and inadequate performance.

The problem is not lack of effort or competence. Application software development is inherently slow and complex. The process of designing, coding, testing, installing, and operating a system involves many meticulous steps. Shortcuts are routes to disaster. Once in place, a system must be updated constantly to meet new business needs and changes in regulation, accounting, or reporting. The costs of this maintenance may be one to three times the original development cost.

Backlogs of approved development projects are frequently so large that it would take two or three years to catch up if no new requests for applications were approved during that time. In 1990, the IS department of one major bank developed an entirely new application every three weeks and made at least one major enhancement to existing applications each day. "The business can't get these systems from us fast enough," observed the head of IS. "I wish we could get them out faster, but there are no quick fixes, especially in testing."

Today, a growing share of application development is being handled outside the IS function and without the involvement of specialized programmers. Development tools such as fourth-generation languages (4GLs) and application generators, software systems that create application programs from a description of a business problem, are enabling business units to do more and more of their own application development, although mainly for smaller systems.

An application package, a general-purpose system from which a firm chooses among optional routines, is an attractive alternative to custom-developed applications. It is particularly effective for generic applications that are common to many companies. A payroll package, for example, will provide a range of prewritten state tax calculations. The user specifies which one applies and which of the available reports are to be produced. Needs not accommodated by a package may be provided by modifying the package or developing additional customized application software. Information systems professionals often refer to the 80-20 rule with respect to packages: users get 80 percent of what they need for 20 percent of the time and effort that would be required to custom develop it. How important is it to get 100 percent?

Tools such as fourth-generation languages and application generators are appealing, given the cost, time, skill base, and complexity associated with application development. But much development still must be done in terms of defining business requirements, creating a customized software system design, and programming, testing, and installing the system. General purpose packages and application generators incur substantial overhead to translate user specifications into detailed processing steps. These tools tend to be best suited to relatively small applications that have generic, firm-independent characteristics (e.g., report generation and small-business general ledger accounting) or to larger well-understood and stable applications common to a business function that requires little, if any, adaptation to company-specific procedures.

Improving software productivity is a major priority for IS units. The pace and quality of application development increasingly affects key aspects of business innovation. Demand for new systems continues to outstrip the ability of IS units to respond. Typically, only 10–20 percent of the programming resource in an IS department is available for developing new systems; 20–40 percent is usually committed to enhancing existing systems to meet additional business needs and 50–70 percent to maintaining old systems (for example, adapting them to changes in tax laws, organization, processing needs, and so forth).

Many IS units are investing in productivity tools such as CASE (Computer-Aided Software Engineering) to speed up design and implementation. These are personal computer-based software aids that provide a structure to the development process that ensures greater accuracy and consistency. Some companies report significant productivity gains from CASE, but there is as yet no evidence that it solves the ongoing problems of delivering large-scale applications on time, within budget, and without errors.

There is no quick fix to the application software bottleneck. Managers should not look for a panacea, nor should they listen to anyone who says, "But it's easy...here's our magic tool." There are no magic solutions to application development problems, and the success of its tools can be highly circumstance specific. Application development is likely to remain a major problem for companies throughout the coming decade.

See also: *Bug, Computer-Aided Software Engineering, Package, Programming, Prototyping, Maintenance, Systems Life Cycle*

Architecture   One of the central concepts in the organizational evolution of IT, architecture refers to a technical blueprint for evolving a corporate infrastructure resource that can be shared by many users and services. The three main elements of an architecture are themselves often referred to individually as architectures.

The IT architecture is the strategy, not the applications built within that architecture. The architecture determines the firm's practical range of technical options and thus increasingly its business options. Do you know your organization's architecture? Your customers'? Your competitors'? You should.

- The processing systems architecture defines the technical standards for the hardware, operating systems environment, and applications software needed to handle the full spectrum of a firm's information-processing requirements. Standards are formats, procedures, and interfaces that ensure that equipment and software from a range of vendors will work together.

- The telecommunications (or network) architecture defines the linkages among a firms' communications facilities over which information moves within the organization and to and from other organizations. It, too, depends on standards.

- The data architecture, by far the most complex of the three architectures and the most difficult to implement, defines the organization of data for purposes of cross-referencing and retrieval, and the creation of an information resource that can be accessed by a wide range of business applications.

The three subarchitectures fit together to provide the corporate master architecture, the blueprint by which a firm's separate IT resources can be integrated. The alternative to developing an architecture—choosing the technology base best suited to a specific application using such criteria as cost, efficiency, speed, and ease of use—is a sensible strategy only if business applications need not fit together in order to share data or telecommunications resources. As soon as they do, an architecture becomes essential.

Given the enormous variety of services and equipment that must be integrated, the technical details involved in defining and implementing an architecture are extraordinarily complex. Most firms' information technology facilities cover a wide range of incompatible systems that have been built up over many years. Standards are a very recent development in the IT field, and most hardware, operating systems, and telecommunications services are still unique to single vendors. Many companies are choosing to wait until the needed standards are fully implemented before defining a blueprint for integration. They are ill-advised to do so. However difficult the task of rationalizing a multivendor mess and moving toward integration is today, it will be even more so tomorrow.

The need for an architecture is driven by widespread "incompatibility" among existing computer and telecommunications and data formats and by the lack of an accepted set of complete, proven, and stable IT standards. Many standards have been defined but few are fully implemented and their interpretation and implementation in products vary widely, effectively rendering them nonstandard standards.

An effective architecture must satisfy three, often conflicting, requirements: (1) that it provide as much vendor-independence as practical (firms are increasingly hesitant to adopt "proprietary" systems that can be provided by only one vendor); (2) that it be capable of rationalizing the frequent multivendor, multitechnology chaos of incompatible elements (a given company may have built its financial applications on IBM systems, its engineering applications on hardware and operating systems unique to Digital Equipment Corporation, Hewlett-Packard, Prime, or Sun, its office technology applications on Wang or Data General products, and its data-base management software, local area networks, and data communications facilities on a wide variety of vendors' facilities; it is not unusual for a firm to have from 10 to 40 incompatible networks and from 5 to 50 incompatible processing systems); and (3) that it incorporate the standards being adopted or likely to be adopted by leading vendors and electronic trading partners.

The need for a comprehensive set of vendor-independent standards is increasingly being recognized by vendor and user communities alike. What is needed is the equivalent of what has evolved in the electrical utilities industry: standardized interfaces such as the three-pin plug into the wall socket; standardized voltages, specifications for light bulb fittings, and so on. The Open Systems Interconnection model, or OSI, is the internationally accepted framework for evolving a complete and open set of such standards.

Although there has been a tendency to advance OSI as the long-term solution to integration, defining and implementing an architecture can take years, possibly even a decade. IS planners must be very selective in balancing the combination of standards that preserve existing investments with those that increase openness.

Conceptually, architectures and open standards are deceptively simple. Managers need to be aware that the tidy diagrams hide a morass of technical details, uncertainties, and, above all, existing incompatibilities. Nevertheless, developments in standards, particularly the convergence of IBM and many of its most effective competitors on compatibility with both key IBM architectures and key vendor-independent standards (notably OSI and UNIX), are easing the architect's task.

The firm that does not have an IT architecture does not have a real IT strategy. The architecture is the strategy. It determines the practical range of applications the firm can develop, which, in turn, determines the practical range of business and product strategies it may choose among. Business planners and many business managers are also well advised to know their key customers' and competitors' architectures.

See also: *Compatibility, Integration, Open Systems Interconnection, Platform, Standards*

Artificial Intelligence (AI)   Artificial Intelligence, or AI, is the

study of how to represent human intelligence in ways that permit the development of computer hardware and software systems that can act as decision makers. This is one of the most promising, if overhyped, longer term directions of effort for exploiting computers.

The evolution of AI has followed two distinct tracks. The first has been to create computer systems that mimic human thought processes in order to solve general problems. Chess playing programs have been the main measure of progress here, with proponents of AI arguing that as soon as an AI program beats the human world champion we will at last have computers that "think." There are strong bodies of both support for and opposition to that claim among philosphers and computer scientists.

The second approach combines the best thinking of experts in a piece of software designed to solve specific problems. So-called expert systems have been most successfully applied to aspects of decision making that principally involve recognizing and responding to recurring patterns. The expert's knowledge is coded as "rules," which typically take the form of "if ...then ...else" statements (for example: if condition A applies, then make inference B, else move on to C). Expert systems have been developed in such diverse areas as robotics in manufacturing, financial planning, medical diagnosis, credit risk assessment, chemical analysis, and oil and mineral exploration.

The fledgling AI industry that grew up in the 1980s, although it greatly underestimated the difficulty of "knowledge representation" and "knowledge engineering," has nevertheless turned out many practical, if highly specialized and expensive, tools for software development. Notable among these are expert system "shells," which provide an organizing framework for developing software targeted at a specific decision task such as troubleshooting a steam turbine generator or a diesel locomotive engine.

The greatest obstacle to progress in AI has been the inability to "teach" a computer to recognize and adapt to context and to use what we call common sense, something computers entirely lack. How can a computer recognize the difference between a hole in the ground and a dark shadow? How can it infer the difference between the following sentences: "Time flies like an arrow" and "Fruit flies like a banana"?

A high point of AI came in 1956 when a computer program, Logic Theorist, proved several theorems in Whitehead and Russell's **Principia Mathematica.** *Its creators then claimed that "there are now in the world machines that think, learn and create." They predicted that the world chess champion would be a computer before the end of the 1970s. That has not happened, but the Deep Thought program missed a chance to draw a game with Anatol Karpov in 1990—because it was too dumb to spot that it could draw but not win.*

Progress in AI will, in the aggregate, be driven by developments in psychology, linguistics, computer science, and hardware technology. Expert systems development will be paced by the sensible choice of decision tasks and realistic expectations of what can be accomplished.

See also: Decision Support System, Expert Systems

ASCII   See American Standard Code for Information Interchange

ATM   See Automated Teller Machine

Automated Teller Machine   Automated teller machines, or ATMs, have become a basic access point for banking services. An ATM system comprises (1) specialized, card-accessed workstations (the ATMs); (2) remote computers that store and update customer records and authorize and execute transactions; and (3) the telecommunications links between the ATMs and the remote computers. The range of technical and competitive options within and across these elements is broad.

A bank may decide to build its own ATM network or to share development and operational costs with a consortium of banks. It may design its systems to link to such other services as credit card providers' or retailers' networks. It may "distribute" functions to the ATM in order to reduce both the workload on the central computer and the amount of telecommunications between it and the ATM. For example, the software that displays options and guides the card owner through the procedures can reside in the ATM; only when the transaction involves the need to check whether the customer has enough funds to cover a withdrawal does control need to be passed to the remote computer.

There are several general lessons managers can learn from the history of ATMs that are relevant today to strategies for such major IT-based business initiatives as point of sale, electronic data interchange, computer-integrated manufacturing, and image processing. In the decade in which ATMs changed the basis of customer service, banks have had to address primarily two competitive issues: whether to lead or to follow the leaders; and whether to compete by installing an ATM system that accepts only one's own cards or by sharing services and facilities with other banks and nonbank service providers.

Many commentators question whether the early leaders in ATMs gained any real competitive advantage; as the laggards caught up, customer demand pressured more and more banks to accept one another's cards and all banks to find a way of providing what is now the electronic equivalent of the checkbook. They argue that the industry as a whole would have gained more by cooperating rather than competing.

Though it is subject to many valid counterarguments, this view highlights the managerial importance of continued attention to the two sets of questions that dominate competitive positioning through information technology: (1) When should we lead and when should we follow? Is it important that we move ahead fast to ensure that we are not preempted by competitors? Or are we better off waiting until the technology and application are proven, thereby reducing our risk? (2) When should we compete and when should we cooperate? Is this an area in which it will pay off to have our own systems? Or should we share costs and resources with other firms within or outside our industry?

There are no easy answers to these questions. Moving too early risks failure; moving too late risks loss of business to competitors. If catching up involves a lead time of two to five years, as it often does, waiting may result in a sustained competitive disadvantage.

One useful way to address the issue of timing in the competitive use of IT is to look ahead five years and ask questions: (1) Is this business service likely to be a competitive necessity then? If so, by when must we have begun our move to be there when demand takes off? (2) Is this a competitive opportunity today? If so, what is the likely payoff from getting there ahead of the competition? How long an advantage in years are we likely to obtain? (3) How long can we afford to wait?

The principal technical issues associated with ATMs relate to security, reliability, and efficiency. From the customer's perspective, efficiency is indicated by response time: how fast the ATM responds when a key is hit. Adding a tenth of a second to each transaction can create unacceptable delays in a network with 50,000 customers simultaneously trying to make withdrawals and deposits. Reliability and

The ATM does nothing "new" or "innovative" but it has transformed the nature of banking. A radical idea in 1977, when Citibank pioneered the ATM, it was an interesting competitive opportunity in 1980 and an absolute competitive necessity by 1983. IT can change the competitive dynamics of an industry when it changes the base level of service and convenience.

security are obviously essential, but they are also technically complex and costly.

See also: Network, Point of Sale, Telecommunications

Baby Bell   See Regional Bell Operating Company

Backbone Network   A backbone network is a key managerial, as well as technical, concept. The physical locations of information stores and information needs are often very different in a large organization. To get information from where it is stored to where it is needed, a company relies on networks. A large organization will often use a number of different networks, some of which may not be connected to others. A backbone network is the completion of the routes among all of an organization's networks, extant and anticipated.

A backbone network, like the interstate highway system, is not intended to connect two points, but rather to provide a high-speed corridor that is common to many points. Entering the system from a connector route, one can use as little or as much of the length of the corridor as is needed to get to the destination connector route. While on it, one is afforded the advantage of fast travel on a broad surface and efficient routing though complex exchanges. These correspond, in a backbone network, to high bandwidth and advanced switching technology, respectively.

Defining an effective corporate backbone network can be easier conceptually and even technically than politically. To overcome resistance from business units that have extant networks and see no benefits in change, a firm needs a corporate telecommunications planner with the clout to establish policies and standards and ensure that they are adhered to. The economic and technical advantages that accrue to all business units from the implementation of a corporate backbone network are generally sufficiently compelling to warrant surmounting whatever obstacles emerge.

See also: Data Communications, International Telecommunications, Network, Telecommunications

Designing a corporate telecommunications infrastructure is analogous to designing a transportation system. The backbone network corresponds to the main highways, with local exits and rotaries.

Backup and Recovery Computers and telecommunications systems are susceptible to damage from a variety of sources, including power loss, hardware problems, and so forth. In general, computer systems operate at a level of reliability that well exceeds 99 percent. Unfortunately, that is not good enough for companies that depend on on-line transaction processing for key elements of operations and customer service. For such companies, when the system is down, so is the business.

Routine protection against system failures, or "crashes," can be provided by copying, or "backing up," data files. How frequently a backup is made depends upon how critical it is not to lose transactions or to have to reprocess them. The more time-critical the business process, the more frequent the backup. Personal computer users often learn too late the importance of backing up their hard disk files.

A few computer vendors offer "nonstop" on-line transaction processing systems, in which multiple systems process data in parallel. If one fails, the others continue processing and no data is lost. Many airlines, banks, and retailers that rely on point-of-sale processing use such nonstop systems, which are the distinctive market niche of Tandem Computers and Stratus.

Recovery from a system failure can be either quick, involving a "hot" restart that is automatic and so fast that users may not notice loss of service, or lengthy, requiring a "cold" restart in which the entire system is reloaded using the backup data files. Hot restarts can be provided by running two processors in different locations. When one crashes, the other's operating system immediately takes over. Telecommunications networks accomplish the equivalent of this approach through automated network management software that continuously monitors transmission flows through the system and reroutes traffic if a line is down or a piece of equipment fails. The network design that ensures that there are alternative paths through the network takes planning and can add expense.

Firms vary widely in the provisions they make to handle disasters. Some make none. They have a single computer center with a single transmission line coming into it. If the line is cut, they hope it will be repaired soon. When the computer is down, they hope the vendor's

New York City processes $1.5 trillion of financial transactions a day, yet only 15 percent of the firms involved have any backup capabilities. If their telephone systems or computers go down, all they can do is send people home. When this happens, their business strategy is now suddenly and completely irrelevant.

systems engineers will get it back up quickly. Given the high level of reliability of today's computers and telecommunications systems, this is often an acceptable strategy. But it is a dangerous risk if a company's cash flow, customer service, and business reputation depend greatly on its on-line processing systems.

See also: Network Management, Security

Bandwidth was the binding constraint on what types of information could be transmitted efficiently until satellites and fiber optics multiplied speeds by a factor of 200,000 in a decade. The 1980s saw the personal computer revolution and ushered in the bandwidth revolution.

Bandwidth   Bandwidth is a measure of the carrying capacity of a telecommunications link. It determines the speed at which information can be transmitted, how much information can share the link, and, consequently, the practical range of the applications it can support.

Although generally expressed in terms of "bits per second" (bps), bandwidth technically refers, as for radio and television, to the usable range of frequencies of the transmission signal (e.g., kilohertz, megahertz, and gigahertz).

Voice-grade analog telephone lines typically transmit information at up to 9,600 bits per second, which is sufficient for applications such as electronic mail. (At 1,200 bits per second, a typed page takes about 12 seconds to transmit, which is acceptable to most casual users; transmitting complex engineering diagrams and large data files would take an unacceptably long time at these speeds.)

Microwave (and satellite) transmission speeds range from 1.544 to 45 million bps and local area networks typically run at between 2 and 16 Mbps (millions of bits per second). Fiber optics links currently transmit at rates of from 100 Mbps to 2.4 Gbps (billions of bits per second). (At 720 Mbps, the entire works of Shakespeare could be transmitted in a quarter of a second!) SONET (synchronous optical network) transmits data at 2.4 Gbps. AT&T is the driving force for SONET, which was first implemented by the Chicago Teleport in early 1991.

In terms of volume, the equivalent of the number of telephone calls that can be handled simultaneously by each of these media range from 4 to 240 for telephone wire, to 5,000 for coaxial cable, to 8,000–15,000 for microwave, to more than 100,000 for fiber optic cable.

Bandwidth has historically been expensive and scarce. Today, it is cheap and plentiful. High-speed digital communication offers tremendous economies of advanced technology and scale. It also makes practical entirely new uses of telecommunications in business. The old systems could not transmit high-resolution images of documents, for instance, at an acceptable cost and speed. Fiber-based transmission can send voice, image, video, or data quickly and accurately and increasingly inexpensively.

See also: Fiber Optics, Megahertz and Gigahertz, Network, Satellite, Transmission

Bar Code   Bar coding is becoming the most effective way to capture sales and inventory information. Bar codes can be read far more quickly by a scanner device than they could be keyed into a computer or even read by the human eye. For this reason, they are turning up in unlikely places. Long common on groceries and magazines, bar codes are turning up on railroad cars, parts destined for assembly, and all manner of products. In Europe, trucks driving between France and Germany have begun to display on their windows bar coded information about licenses, customs clearances, and freight. A customs official can aim a bar code reader at the truck, immediately see if it has the necessary clearances, and wave it through as the driver downshifts to second gear. Portable scanning devices, hand-held computers, and even radio devices can quickly read and input the information from bar codes into computer processing systems for point-of-sale pricing, updating inventory and delivery records, tracking physical movements of goods, invoicing, and so forth.

A bar code is nothing more than an electronic tag; the technique is as applicable to insurance application forms as to supermarket items. Bar coding enables a company to capture information as events happen, move it quickly into central data bases, and feed it back in the form of selective summaries and reports that alert people in the field, planning staff, and corporate management. Documents as well as physical goods can be tracked as they move through a business process without extra paperwork or bureaucracy or manual keying of data.

See also: Hand-Held Computer, Image Technology, Point of Sale, On-Line Transaction Processing

Bar codes move the information with the goods—or the form, or the person, or the truck. A scanner can read the bar code faster than the human eye can read numbers. The width of each bar indicates a number from 0–9.

One of the largest financial service firms in the United States discovered in May 1990 that it had incorrectly overstated its foreign exchange profit for April by $45 million. It handled the FX trades on-line, but the accounting and payment records were processed month-ly, by batch; someone made an error in the paperwork so the trading and accounting records were out of sync. Batch processing is the most efficient and cheapest way to operate. It is not the most effective though.

Batch Processing   Batch processing is the oldest established way of operating computers. Batch processing takes its name from the "batching" of transactions; orders, payments, and time sheets, for example, are accumulated over a period of time, such as a day, week, or month and then processed in a single computer run.

Batch processing incurs lower costs and overhead and is more efficient and less expensive than on-line transaction processing. It is far more economical to store large volumes of data off-line on tape than on-line, and because they are typically processed in sequence, data such as employee records can be organized so as to ensure the simplest and fastest updating of master files. Batch processing also generally affords a wide enough time window to accommodate reruns in the event of major system errors. Should the computer "crash," a service bureau may be able to provide a machine to run the batch system. Security is another strength of batch systems; the data centers are typically off limits, and the only way transactions get into the system is through the user departments. The principal shortcomings of batch processing are the information gap that results from the time lag between the processing and reporting of transactions, and that puts a firm's internal operational needs ahead of the customers' service needs.

Although rapidly being replaced by on-line transaction processing, a more expensive and complex but increasingly essential requirement for more and more business activities, batch processing remains a practical alternative for many traditional business functions. Obviously, an airline reservation system is not a candidate for batch processing. Travel agents would have to wait until the next day for a response to their requests and airline managers and planning staff would be a day behind in operating information. For payroll, the situation is quite different. Transactions—pertaining, for example, to hours worked, absences, salary increases, overtime, and so forth—do not have to be processed immediately but can be accumulated and then sorted, checked for errors, and processed literally as a batch at the end of the month. Batch processing keeps costs and overhead low. Off-line storage on tape is far cheaper than keeping large volumes of data on-line. Since all the employee records need to be processed in sequence, the transaction data can be organized and records sorted to ensure the simplest and fastest updating of master file records.

Ten years ago, almost all banks processed customer checking account deposits and withdrawals through batch systems, daily for transactions, monthly for statements, and annually for tax records. Automated teller machines have moved more and more transactions on-line, although check processing, monthly statements, and tax accounting continue to be handled in batch mode.

Batch processing will survive through the century, but every system that is part of just-in-time business and customer service is likely to move on-line well before then.

See also: On-Line, On-line Transaction Processing

Bits and Bytes　A bit is the fundamental unit of coding by which information is represented digitally. A bit is either "on" or "off," signifying the presence or absence of an electrical signal, which is the only thing a computer can store. A 1 is typically used to code an "on" bit, a 0 to code an "off" bit. A set of eight bits, termed a byte, represents one "character," such as "W," "j," "5," or "#."

Any form of information—voice, text, graphics, color photographs, and television pictures—can be reduced to combinations of bits and stored in a computer or transmitted over telecommunications lines. The magnificent photographs of Jupiter and Saturn and their moons that were relayed to earth by Voyager were in digital form. So is the music on a compact disc.

A computer's storage capacity is generally measured in bytes and a telecommunications facility's information-moving capability in bits per second. As a point of interest, approximate sizes in bits of selected types of messages and transactions are given below.

A credit authorization request: **1,000 bits**

An electronic mail message (1 page): **5,000**

Digital voice (1 second): **56,000**

Digital facsimile (1 page): **100,000**

Full motion video (one second, TV quality): **10,000,000**

Bits and bytes are the background for what IT professionals call

Computers code all information or instructions as ones and zeroes, which represent on and off electrical signals. A single character, such as "a," "$," or ">" is coded as a combination of eight bits, called a byte. A color photograph may require hundreds of thousands of bits to code it. The speed of telecommunications transmission is indicated in bits per second, and the size of a computer software program or data base in bytes.

"voice/data/text/image integration." When all these are coded in bits, the telephone system becomes a vehicle for carrying any type of information into the home and office. This is the goal of Integrated Services Digital Network (ISDN), the telephone service providers' grand plan for the 1990s that will enable a firm's telecommunications highway to carry voice and data simultaneously, with many opportunities for reducing costs and improving efficiency. Image processing technology will be used to handle documents, checks, photographs, recorded phone calls, handwritten letters, and conventional computer transactions and data as if all were the same medium.

Humans see photographs as different from telephone messages and handwritten memos as different from memos produced by a word processor. These distinctions are meaningless to computers, which simply manipulate ones and zeros. Computers process bits, digital communications facilities move them. The significance of what bits represent is lost to these electronic contrivances.

See also: Data, Digital

Bridges, Routers, and Gateways Bridges, routers and gateways are used to connect telecommunications networks to one another. Bridges and routers are used to link local area networks that use the same communication "protocol." The latter has the added ability to select the fastest, least-congested, and least-expensive route between two networks. Gateways are more complex devices capable of converting message formats and communication protocols in order to link dissimilar networks.

There are so many different types of telecommunications equipment and modes of transmission that a whole industry has emerged to interconnect them.

Bridges, routers, and gateways and other types of converters add overhead, are a source of performance problems, and create bottlenecks. They are also expensive. In late 1991, a bridge cost between $2,000 and $9,000, a router between $10,000 and $20,000. Gateways are even more expensive.

Much of the use of converters derives from the lack of an information architecture. Personal computer facilities and the local area networks that connect them have proliferated on a case-by-case basis in many large firms. Scant attention was been paid to the need to link these systems for purposes of sharing corporate information or telecommunications facilities. There was little effort to develop transportation policies for information. It is an iron law of IT that today's stand-alone system is tomorrow's networked system and that today's functionally or departmentally based application will tomorrow almost surely, for business reasons, need to link to other services and facilities inside and outside the organization. Together, bridges, gateways, and routers play an important role in corporate communications and computing, but it should be a small one.

See also: Protocol, Switch, Telecommunications

Bug   A bug is an error. Because large-scale software systems are extraordinarily complex, it is practically impossible to anticipate every potential combination of circumstances that will arise in their use. Consequently, they can never be proven to be bug-free or guaranteed to produce perfect results all the time, however rigorously they might be tested.

Most business computer systems are compilations of relatively simple processing rules that involve little mathematics. But the rules must be complete, consistent, and precisely sequenced. Tiny differences or oversights can wreck a process, with expensive business consequences. For example, a small and overlooked miscalculation in American Airlines' yield management system, the best in the industry, led to discount fares being cut off too early. This bug, which went undetected for several months, cost the airline $50 million. The programs appeared to work correctly; the error was subtle. In another instance, the sequence in which a spreadsheet program added numbers yielded an analysis that indicated that the firm should acquire a company, which it did. Later suspicions that the numbers were faulty led to the discovery that switching the sequence in which the calculations were made clearly indicated that the acquisition would be a disaster. That bug cost $12 million.

Managers may be interested in a bug that is patiently waiting until January 1, 2000, to reveal itself. Dates in computer records are stored in as compact a form as possible to save space and speed up retrieval and processing. There is no need, for example, to store year of birth in a payroll or benefits system as "1945"; "45" is sufficient. But what will happen in the year 2000? The dutiful software will calculate pension and pay for an employee who has turned minus 55 years old (the age calculation is the current year minus birthdate; 2000 minus 1945 will be represented by the software as 00 minus 45). At a conference on the year 2000 "date-dependency" problem held in New York in early 1991, attendees offered such comments as "the impact of the problem hasn't hit top management yet" and "we may not really understand the scope of the date problem." What makes programming such a complex craft is that it requires a quirky way of thinking that can anticipate such vagaries.

The three most expensive known software errors cost the firms involved $1.6 billion, $900 million, and $245 million. Each was the result of changing just one line of code in an existing program. No large software program can be proven not to contain a bug.

Bugs are a reality of IT life. They explain why testing costs more than programming in the systems development life cycle. They also demonstrate the degree to which technology risk is now business risk. When IT was confined mainly to back office operations, the impacts of bugs could generally be hidden from customers. Today, with more of the basics of customer service, quality, and logistics on-line, situations like the following are becoming all too common.

> Thousands of Sovran Bank customers looking for pocket money from the bank's automated teller machines yesterday started the weekend on the wrong foot. The ATMs ate their magnetized cards... "We changed a program, we tested it fully, but something showed up that didn't appear in the tests,"...Technicians corrected the program by early afternoon and branch staffers began mailing the [2,100] captured cards back to their owners, who will have to rely on credit cards and checks for the duration of the weekend. (*Washington Post*, May 13, 1990)

Large software systems involve masses of detailed definitions of procedures, calculations, and data. The Air Force calculates that 5,000 pages of documentation are needed to specify the "requirements" for a program of 100,000 lines of code. The logistics system for the F-15 fighter will contain more than three million lines of code for more than 4,000 discrete processes in nearly 70 programs. Many *Fortune* 1000 firms' existing processing systems for manufacturing, distribution, ordering, and customer service are comparable in scale and often contain very old, generally undocumented elements that become harder and harder to maintain.

The best remedy for bugs is to improve the quality of the software development discipline through the use of such emerging tools and techniques as Computer-Aided Software Engineering (CASE), structured methods, data-base management systems, and object-oriented programming systems (OOPS). IS units must also avoid caving in to business unit pressures to cut corners in systems development because of budget and time pressures, and encourage sustained and meaningful involvement by people who understand the application being worked on and can anticipate and know how to handle exceptions and special cases.

Using CASE tools, the Air Force cut error rates in a major operational system from 8 to 4 errors per thousand lines of code. For a business that has one million lines of program code in use, that improvement translates to a 4,000 instead of 8,000 potential disasters in customer service and the reliability of business operations per year. A 1991 MIT study concluded that the typical domestic program experiences 4.4 technical failures per thousand lines of source code in the first twelve months of use. The corresponding figure for Japanese-developed programs is estimated to be less than two.

See also: Application Software and Application Development, Computer-Aided Software Engineering, Maintenance

Business Television   Business television is an alternative to memos and the corporate communications department's glossies for supporting management-staff communication and getting word out to the broader organization. It can be surprisingly inexpensive to provide, being just another type of traffic on the corporate communications network. A firm that has installed small satellite dishes at its stores and principal dealer locations to handle, say, on-line transaction processing already has the basis for providing business television. K mart, for instance, calculates that the full cost for its business television via satellite is 50 cents an hour per store.

Business television differs from videoconferencing in being a one-way video medium, although generally a two-way audio link is provided to support questions and discussion. This makes the medium valuable for management presentations, training, and news updates.

With "communication," "partnership," and "teamwork" widely espoused organizational priorities for the 1990s, business television is a tool for organizational advantage. Its adoption is most often impeded by virtue of its not fitting the typical Information Systems organization's responsibilities and capabilities. Thus it must often rely on "championing" by an influential business manager.

A number of leading companies have set examples in the effective use of business television. Federal Express's founder and chairman, Fred Smith, is a strong believer in its value in keeping employees in touch with what is happening in the company and ensuring that they never hear important news about the company from the press before they hear it from their own management. Digital Equipment Corporation's chairman, Ken Olsen, uses business television in project and management meetings to personalize his leadership. Olsen argues that the ability to bring teams together electronically will be a major source of organizational advantage in a world of just-in-time everything. The head of Domino's Pizza believes that business television helps both to keep people informed and well-trained and to keep the corporate headquarters staff small, flexible, and responsive to the field.

See also: Videoconferencing

The chairman of K mart regularly uses the firm's television network to talk to staff across 2,200 stores simultaneously and answer their questions. "The satellite is fantastic," he said. "I would never believe it. You walk into a store and it's like they've known you for 15 years."

Byte   See Bits and Bytes

Cables, Plugs, and Sockets   Lack of standardization in the IT field is perhaps most clearly illustrated by the plethora of cables, plugs, and sockets needed to tie IT devices together. Imagine if connecting a VCR to a television set required choosing between 22 types of cable, depending on the make of the VCR and TV. That is precisely the number of cable sockets that appeared in a recent trade press advertisement for a telecommunications provider. They were identified as "standard."

Few senior managers ever visit their organization's data centers and fewer still ever view the tangled black and gray spaghetti beneath the floor panels that interconnect the quiet cabinets and consoles that comprise the corporate computer system. The schematics that vendors and consultants draw to illustrate integration and interconnection are one thing; the cables, plugs, and sockets required to achieve them are quite another.

There is an apocryphal, but plausible, story of a company that had so many undocumented cables running through its walls and under its floors to connect personal computers, word processors, telephones, and computers that it finally sold the building, with the cables intact, and moved into new quarters to start over. Simply moving a person's telephone with his or her desk had become an effort taking weeks, and local area network installation and upgrading had become major logistical projects. The company knew neither where all the cables were, nor how many there were. It had managed its computers, but not the cables that interconnected them.

One implication of the myriad of connectors involved in even a fairly simple IT facility is that buildings now need to be explicitly designed for computer and telecommunications use. Such "intelligent" buildings include central shafts and underfloor space for cables, backup power supplies, and, in some cases, built-in fiber optic links.

See also: *Compatibility, Connectivity, Network*

"5,739 Solutions...In just one year, we designed and built over 18,000 custom cables"— from a 1991 advertisement by Black Box Corporation

CAD/CAM   See Computer-Aided Design/Computer-Aided Manufacturing

CASE   See Computer-Aided Software Engineering

CCITT   See Consultative Committee for International Telephony and Telegraphy

CD-ROM   See Compact Disc-Read Only Memory

Cellular Communication   Cellular communication is a form of mobile communication involving the use of a wireless, radio-frequency telephone that allows calls to be made from a car or while walking along a sidewalk as long as the caller is within what is termed a statistical metropolitan area, or SMA. Located within each SMA are radio base stations that are capable of sending and receiving telephone calls over short distances. The broadcasting range around this base constitutes a

The industry is positioning for the next generation of cellular, called PCN—Personal Communications Networks. In April 1991, the FCC established a "pioneer's preference" regulation, to grant preferential treatment to innovators in wireless technology.

cell. Calls are passed from one cell to another as the sender or receiver moves (for example, driving from New York into New Jersey). Calls made to recipients in a noncontiguous SMA or outside of any SMA are connected to local and long-distance telephone systems.

A new generation of digital cellular systems that will replace existing analog systems will increase capacity by a factor of three while reducing operating costs. The cellular communications industry is roughly at the stage the cable television industry was at in the early 1980s and exhibits many of the same trends, problems, and issues — it is not yet making money and lacks the critical mass of subscribers needed to recoup the necessary investments in infrastructure. In the absence of fully defined standards, many facilities are incompatible. State and federal regulators are still defining policy. Given that the FCC is dividing the country up into 300 metropolitan and 420 rural units, it should not be surprising that the industry is highly fragmented geographically. Current FCC strategy for awarding cellular franchises, reminiscent of cable television, is to encourage duopolies consisting of a local consortium or company and an established "non-wireline" telecommunications provider.

Progress in cellular communication has been more rapid in Europe. Scandinavia leads the world in mobile communications, with approximately 5 percent of telephone subscribers also having cellular service, and Germany has taken the lead in promoting a pan-European capability, which should be in place by the mid-1990s. Mobile communication — cellular plus satellite-based systems — will certainly be a key element in Eastern Europe's entry into the world of modern telecommunications, since countries such as Poland and Hungary simply cannot afford the time and costs associated with developing a fixed-network infrastructure.

See also: Mobile Communication, Network, Satellite, Telecommunications, Transmission

Central Processing Unit (CPU) The central processing unit, or CPU, is the chip or set of chips that contains the circuits that process instructions and data stored in a computer's memory. The basic dimensions of power of a CPU are its "clock speed," measured in megahertz (the range of usable electromagnetic frequencies used to move information) and the number of bits of data it can input, store, and process simultaneously. The original Apple II CPU was built on an 8-bit chip. The IBM personal computer used a 16-bit chip. Today, the standard chip is 32 bits.

The number of bits also determines the amount of memory that can be directly "addressed," which, in turn, determines the size of the software programs that can be run. The rate of progress in the development of chips is illustrated in the table below. The period from the introduction of the first chip to the last was eight years.

Manufacturer	Chip	Bits	Directly addressable memory	Notes
Intel	8088	16	1 megabyte	used in the original IBM PC
Intel	80286	16	16 megabytes	5-20 times faster than the 8088
Motorola	68000	32	16 megabytes	used in the Apple Macintosh
Intel	80386	32	4 gigabytes	20-35 times faster than the 8088, allows "multitasking" (running many different programs at the same time)
Intel	80486	32	4 gigabytes *(Megabtyes are millions, gigabytes billions)*	an interim chip with the 586 due in 1992; the design of the 686 is already underway

Classes of computers are increasingly referred to in terms of the generation of chips they use. Managers today are likely to hear about a "386" or a "486" machine. The chip is often more meaningful than the brand in indicating the capabilities of the computer.

Different manufacturers' CPU chips are mutually incompatible in terms of the software they run. The Apple Macintosh and IBM PC versions of the same software package — for example, Microsoft's

When computers were large and expensive, the terms "CPU" and "machine" were equivalent. The CPU is still the core component of any computer, but it is now more equivalent to "chip" than to machine.

MS.WORD — appear to the user exactly the same in terms of functions and commands, but are in fact two entirely different implementations. Each runs on only one CPU under one particular operating system. The Macintosh uses Motorola chips; the IBM PC uses Intel chips.

Intel and Motorola have produced most of the CPU chips used in personal computers and workstations manufactured in the United States. Although Intel dominates the industry today, other firms are matching its rate of innovation. Hewlett-Packard's RISC chip set is the base for its 720 series workstation, which calculates up to ten times faster than a 486-chip personal computer.

Improvements come slowly in software, but not in chips. The 8088 was introduced in 1978, the 80286 in 1984. The 386, the first chip that raised workstation and personal computer capability to what mainframes provided in the mid-1980s, was announced just two years later, in 1986. The cost of the 386 chip in 1991 was just $3 in units of a hundred.

See also: Bits and Bytes, Chip, Host, Mainframe and Minicomputer, Megahertz and Gigahertz, Millions of Instructions per Second

Chargeout and Allocation   Chargeout refers to the allocation of corporate Information Systems organizations' costs to users. It is based on two business principles, one outmoded and ill-guided, the other sensible and vital. The ill-guided notion — that IT being an overhead expense, all central IT costs should be charged out to users — put a leading U.S. university's computing center out of business. The accounting system that required the center to allocate its costs so as to be fully "recovered" on an annual basis employed a simple formula based on connect time (the period of time a user is connected to the service). Because the computer facility was underutilized (subscribers consumed only about 40 percent of its resources), its full cost was spread over a narrow base of users. The resulting chargeout rate was extraordinarily high, as if a restaurant charged $750 for a hamburger because it had only 12 customers. The high chargeout rate drove away more customers, which drove the rate higher and discouraged still more customers until the center was forced to close.

At another university, the computer center took a different approach to chargeout; it developed elaborate formulas to calculate how much of the computer's resources each user was consuming. The typical hourly cost for this university's system was between $30 and $75. Nevertheless, one particular day a student used the computer for two hours and received a bill for $7,800. The day was Christmas Day; the student was a Moslem and the only user on that day. Because costs were automatically fully allocated, he was charged the entire cost per hour of the system for that period. Welcome to People's Distress Airline of Transylvania; you are the only passenger on our scheduled Flight 9099 to Slovarik — that's $12,680, please.

The alternative to allocation — not to charge out computer use at all, but instead absorb it as a central cost — might have been acceptable when IT was a tiny fraction of expenditures, but not when it is a major and growing percentage of capital investment. IT is not a free good. There must be some basis for pricing it so that it is sensibly used. If there were no charge for electricity, who would bother to turn off the lights?

The critical need in allocating IT costs is to establish a realistic usage fee that (1) facilitates investment in longer-term infrastructures (naive chargeout systems often discourage such investment by making early users pay for the entire resource when usage is still small), (2) establishes a price that spreads the cost over the long term, providing users both a fair deal (in that no user group is charged a disproportionately low price at the expense of other users) and a good deal (in that the internal user is charged a price at least as low, and offered a quality of service at least as high, as could be obtained from an external supplier), and (3) encourages a sensible balance between the development and operation of central, shared services and decentralized decision making (striking this balance is the central issue in managing Information Systems as it shifts from highly centralized, corporate data processing to service-driven support for effective business uses of IT).

How the costs of a corporate Information Services group's operations are charged out to the business units that use its resources is one of the most important factors in determining if it is seen by them as a responsive service unit or an expensive bureaucracy.

Although many firms have established policies that transform the central IS unit into a competitive supplier of IT services that must vie with outside suppliers and hence offer competitive prices and services, there remain areas in which efficient exploitation of technology demands a central, shared processing base and technical support that must be charged out or absorbed centrally. Security, network management, operation of corporate data centers, and many areas of telecommunications — though they may look like overhead to business units that face heavy chargeouts and have little control over them — can provide considerable economies of scale, technology, or expertise.

Many firms' allocation, chargeout, and pricing policies for internal systems impede effective economic decisions about IT investment and use, as evidenced by the preceding examples. Too many financial controllers and accountants are locked into the old paradigm of IT as an overhead expense. Those times are gone, and the mindset must go, too. Developing an effective strategy in this area is a key management-policy need.

See also: Cost of IT

Chief Information Officer (CIO)

Chief information officer, or CIO, is the fashionable term for the manager of the corporate Information Systems function. On the positive side, it signals recognition of IT as a major business resource that requires a new type of executive. On the negative side, the title has often been introduced into organizations without the changes needed in the management process to make the role meaningful, the job practical, and the individual effective.

The CIO's role is to coordinate the firm's corporate IT strategy and to ensure that IT is viewed as a competitive as well as an operational resource. Coordination is not the same as control. Traditional data processing departments are notorious for their perceived (and often real) efforts to maintain a monopoly on IT decision making, viewing themselves as both guardian of the technical resource and the only qualified source of expertise and opinion. This has begun to change, as first personal computers and then local area networks facilitated decentralizaton of hardware, software, local communications, and even many aspects of development. Business units that recognize the business importance of IT, and that have felt poorly served by unresponsive central data processing groups, increasingly want to bring IT resources into their own sphere of operation and decision making.

The CIO's job is to encourage such decentralization while ensuring that infrastructure facilities and services remain centrally planned and coordinated, and that the process does not lead to systems disintegration. His or her primary responsibility is to guarantee the integrity of the corporate architecture, promote economies of expertise, and identify critical corporate standards that will ensure that disparate and decentralized development is consistent with the overall needs of the firm. Network management, R&D, vendor strategy and relationships, data and telecommunications architectures and standards, security, the piloting of new technologies, data center consolidation, and strategic application development are all within the purview of the CIO.

The CIO position is a relationship, not a job. If the CIO/top management team relationship is effective, the title doesn't matter. If it is ineffective, the title doesn't matter.

In many ways, the CIO is a relationship rather than a job. The relationship is with the business leadership of the firm. For IT to be used effectively as a business resource, there must be real dialogue and joint planning. Yet in many firms, the CIO is isolated from business discussions but still expected to work competitive wonders, with little if any meaningful direction from the top. It is for this reason that *Business Week* in 1990 described CIO as standing for "Career Is Over"; many CIOs have been unable to balance all the needs and constraints of central versus decentralized development and operations, funding of infrastructures, cost allocations, systems development, and getting demonstrable competitive payoff from IT. They are being fired, according to *Business Week*, at twice the rate of other corporate executives.

"I wear two hats," explained one top CIO. "Under my customer service hat, I encourage every move toward making business units autonomous and putting them in charge of their own destiny; under my corporate hat, I make sure that autonomy doesn't put the company at risk. I am sometimes the good guy and sometimes the bad guy. If I were always to try to be the good guy, I am sure the company would end up with technical chaos. If I were always the bad guy, I'd get fired because I'd be blocking the businesses from getting the technology they must have to compete effectively."

Just as IT is no longer overhead but often the largest single element in a firm's capital investment, the manager of the IT function is no longer a staff administrator and planner, but a new style of line executive. IT is today part of the direct responsibility of top management; it is not something to be delegated and largely ignored.

See also: *Architecture, Platform, Security, Standards*

Chip   Chips — or more properly, microchips — are made of a thin wafer of silicon about 1/16 inch square and 1/30 inch thick. The manufacture of chips, which consist of many layers onto which electronic circuits one hundred times thinner than a human hair are etched, involves as many as 200 discrete steps.

Miniaturization of circuits reduces the distance electricity must travel and thus speeds processing. Packing more circuits onto a chip reduces the cost per unit of computing power. Initial versions of chips are very expensive to design and produce, but as production yields increase with experience (the well-known manufacturing "learning curve"), chips become relatively inexpensive. Today's advanced chip is tomorrow's commodity.

There are two main types of chips, logic chips and memory chips. Logic chips are the basis for the central processing units that execute instructions and perform calculations in computers. Memory chips provide the random access memory (RAM) used to store programs and data. Other specialized chip types include ones that preserve the contents of memory when electrical power is switched off or interrupted, notably EPROM (electrically programmable read-only memory) and EEPROM (electrically erasable PROM), and a recent variety of highly reliable logic chips, called RISC (reduced instruction set computing) chips, that simplify the design of hardware architectures. RISC chips are especially suited to the development of high performance workstations, such as are used in engineering and scientific applications.

"Innovate or die" is the watchword of the chip industry. The price-performance ratio improves at more than 30 percent a year, with no end in sight. Intel's 1992 586 chip will have twice the power of its 486 chip, introduced in 1989, and will contain 1.2 million transistors.

A decade ago, the United States dominated the memory chip industry, and the typical chip stored 16,000, or 16K, bits of data. (The "K" stands for "kilo," which literally means thousands. In computer storage 1K = 1,024 bits. The reason it is not precisely a thousand is because computers code bits in binary powers of 2, and 2 to the power of 9, 1024, is the closest to a thousand.) Today, competition is more intense and 256K chips are routine, with 1M (mega or million bit) chips in production, and 4M chips in early delivery. Thirty-two megabit chips are out of the lab and should be in production soon. The race is now on to produce 64M chips.

A 1 megabit chip can store the equivalent of 100 double-spaced typewritten pages, a 64 megabit chip the equivalent of 400,000 pages. One to four gigabit chips (1 to 4 billion to 6.4 million pages) are in preliminary research and can be expected within the millenium. The main contenders in the development of ultrahigh-density chips are Toshiba, Hitachi, NEC, and Fujitsu in Japan and IBM in the United States. IBM is well up with the Japanese leaders, but because it needs the chips for its own products, it does not sell them on the open market.

The U.S. Department of Defense-backed Sematech research consortium that is trying to restore the United States' lost preeminence in chip making is engaged in efforts to improve the "printing" of circuits onto silicon and reduce the size of etched lines to 0.35 microns, about one two-hundredth the thickness of a human hair. Because the wave length of ultraviolet light cannot produce such fine patterns, the lithographic devices now in use will need new light sources.

If this sounds "gee whiz," it is. What you see of microtechnology in use in products is already obsolescent. This will be true throughout the 1990s and probably well beyond. Alternative materials such as gallium arsenide promise increased speed and density of circuits per chip and manufacturing advantages (e.g., freedom from impurities).

With annual price-performance improvements in chip technology averaging 20–30 percent, business plans based on current technology have a short life. Many firms adopt an existing technology only to see a cheaper, more powerful technology come along months later. Other firms choose to forgo the benefits of a technology upgrade while they wait for the follow-on technology. A firm's best buffer against the present circumstances is a strong corporate architecture that can provide a framework within which new components can be added and older ones replaced in an evolutionary manner consistent with the pace of technology.

See also: *Bits and Bytes, Central Processing Unit, Digital, Random Access Memory*

CIM   See Computer-Integrated Manufacturing

CIO   See Chief Information Officer

Client/Server Model   The client/server model is an important development in the effective combination of what used to be termed mainframe (or host) computers and personal computers and workstations. Before the availability of powerful workstations (a personal computer with communications is effectively a workstation), mainframe computers handled data processing and information management for users who were connected to them by "dumb" terminals, typewriter-like devices that had no processing or storage capability of their own. As use grew and mainframe capacity was taxed, access became a bottleneck and response time was seriously degraded. Use became disproportionately expensive as mainframes spent much of their time handling trivial operations such as checking the validity of inputs and generating and transmitting an error message.

In the client/server model, a host computer or "server" provides data and services to "client" workstations. The client device handles as many functions as possible, reducing the time spent moving information to and from the server. The server, a mainframe or a minicomputer, handles functions that are not efficiently handled by client machines, such as data base management, security, and automated network management. To exploit the very different comparative advantages of client and server, each must logically share the handling of the elements of a business task. The client handles "front end" computing, including all aspects of organizing data for manipulation and display (e.g., generating graphs and reports); the server supplies the data needs of the client as well as any computing that requires extra machine power or specialized software.

The client/server model, though conceptually simple, is not at all simple technically. It requires new operating systems facilities capable of efficiently and effectively managing and synchronizing the communication flow between clients and servers. Because servers must manage complex data access procedures and high-speed communications, the client/server model increases rather than eliminates the need for mainframe equivalent power for what firms often term "mission critical" applications. The local area networks that support client/server communications add another element of complexity.

Client/server computing exploits increasingly powerful workstations as clients and a wide range of machines, from specialized personal

About 20 million personal computers are now linked to telecommunications local area networks. Each of these is a potential "client" for processing, data, and communications services. Each has its own increasingly powerful applications, data, and communications capabilities. Client/server computing is emerging as an approach to getting the most dynamic and effective combination of personal computers, networks, and the machines and software that act as "servers."

computers and "superserver" minicomputers to massive mainframe computers, as servers. Development on one side of the client/server divide fuels development on the other. Power clients need power servers to keep up with their data and communication needs; power servers open up new applications for power clients. The client/server model is clearly the mainstream for Information Systems development in the 1990s.

See also: Cooperative Processing, Distributed Systems

COBOL   COBOL (Common, Business-Oriented Language) is the computer programming language that has longest served commercial application development. Today, it is viewed as a cumbersome language, and used primarily in large transaction processing systems. Often these are sets of older programs that have been patched and updated over the years, usually without adequate documentation, making them painfully and tediously difficult to maintain.

A very wordy language, COBOL's special strength is the richness of its facilities for describing data items (such as the master records that store customer information). It is probably also the language most widely known among application system developers and remains essential to firms that must maintain existing COBOL systems. More than 90 percent of domestic companies still use COBOL; estimates put the amount of COBOL code in use by U.S. business at about 100 billion lines. Thus we can expect COBOL to still be in use in the year 2001, more than 40 years after it first came into commercial use.

See also: Application Software and Application Development, Programming

Compact Disc-Read Only Memory (CD-ROM)   Compact Disc (CD)-Read Only Memory (ROM) is a form of optical storage. CD-ROM exploits digital coding of information and laser technology to provide fast and flexible searching of large volumes of data. A CD-ROM the size of the compact discs sold in music shops can store more than 100,000 pages of text, and reproduction cost is so low that one firm has found it less expensive to provide manuals on CD-ROM than in printed form.

*There are an estimated 100 billion lines of COBOL code in use today. This cost about $2 trillion to produce. Thirty billion dollars a year is spent by U.S. firms to maintain it. The typical **Fortune** 1000 company maintains 35 million lines of code.*

An F-18 fighter plane weighs 13 tons. So does the documentation that comes with it. The documentation for one commercial airplane comes on CD-ROM and weighs less than 8 ounces.

Sony's late 1990 launch in Japan of a $300 CD-ROM Walkman practically guarantees a massive take-off for a tool that is underused in business. That there has been consistent growth in CD-ROM products and applications in the past five years but no major surge in their use in either business or consumer markets is due largely to the early lack of standards, difficulties in developing indexes to stored information, and a general lack of awareness of the medium among IS professionals and lack of skills and experience among those who are aware of it.

Examples of CD-ROM offerings include the Grolier Encyclopedia for about $200, aerospace manuals (a one-inch stack of CDs replaces literally tons of paper), and many specialized industry and technical data bases that pack masses of abstracts and articles on single discs. Citibank's Collections division, which used to spend hundreds of thousands of dollars on "411" directory assistance phone calls, purchased a CD-ROM that contains a directory of all regional telephone numbers of US West, one of the Bell Operating Companies. The directory is stored on a local area network and accessed by customer service terminals. Hewlett-Packard currently distributes software updates and documentation on CD-ROM (one disc replaces dozens of manuals and can be searched directly from a personal computer), and Disclosure, a Maryland company that has for twenty years published paper and microfiche versions of financial reports filed with the Securities and Exchange Commission, found that many of its customers were willing to pay far more for the CD-ROM version the company now offers because it is less bulky, easier to use, and much faster to access.

A CD-ROM disc reader that attaches to a personal computer costs well under $1,000 and incurs none of the telecommunications costs associated with accessing on-line information services. CD-ROM is a powerful and proven tool for putting masses of information at the fingertips in a form that is easy to scan and digest. Its variants include CD/I (interactive CD, with music and pictures), CD-WORM (write once, read many times) and, in early production at the time this glossary is being written, fully erasable and, hence, fully updatable CD.

Related terms: *Digital, Disk Storage, Image Technology*

Compatibility   Two pieces of hardware (e.g., a personal computer and a printer) are compatible if they can operate together. A software program that runs on a particular operating system is compatible with that operating system. Incompatibility has been the norm in the IT field — computers that don't talk to other computers, communications facilities that can't connect to other communications facilities, printers that work with some computers but not others, software that runs only on specific computers, data bases that will exchange data with some programs but not with others, and different sets of cables for (it seems) every pair of devices that have to be interconnected.

Standards, published specifications of procedures, equipment interfaces, and data formats, are the key to reducing and eventually perhaps eliminating incompatibility. Suppliers that ensure that their telecommunications, hardware, and software products comply with a standard can expect those products to be compatible with the products of other suppliers that have adhered to the same standard.

Two types of standards that help to reduce incompatibility are (1) de facto standards created by the marketplace, and (2) stable standards defined by standard-setting groups that are implemented in the products of a plurality of key suppliers. An example of a de facto standard is MS.DOS, originally a proprietary operating system for the IBM personal computer. When MS.DOS first appeared, there were several competing, and of course incompatible, operating systems on the market; within two years of its debut, the IBM PC dominated the corporate marketplace, leading software suppliers to develop products for the MS.DOS market and hardware manufacturers to ensure that their products were "IBM-compatible." The dragon, incompatibility, was not slain, however. Apple Computer announced its own operating systems for its Macintosh and enthusiasm continues to build for the Bell Laboratories–developed UNIX operating system. Both are incompatible with MS.DOS. Even IBM, when it announced a new generation of personal computers, introduced a new operating system that is incompatible with MS.DOS. Nevertheless, MS.DOS remains the best-established de facto standard in business use and thus the base for the widest range of compatible hardware and software.

Examples of committee-defined standards implemented in real

The costs of incompatibility are large and widely recognized. They are being reduced by progress in implementing standards, but unless business managers understand the causes of incompatibility and why integration is such a priority for Information Services planners, incompatibility is likely to remain the norm; managers will then assess personal computers, local area networks, and software packages on the basis of their individual features instead of their compatibility with other elements of the firm's IT base.

products include the vendor-independent Ethernet (for local area networks), X.25 (for international telecommunications), and IBM's SNA (Systems Network Architecture), which, though proprietary, is stable and documented in a manner that permits competitors to interface their products to it.

It will be decades before incompatibility ceases to be a significant impediment to effective IT use. The primary goal of an IT architecture is to move away from incompatibility toward integration by evolving a business platform for delivering IT services, sharing information and resources, and integrating business functions. As a technical barrier, incompatibility is irksome; when it becomes a business barrier, it can cost an organization dearly.

See also: Architecture, Connectivity, Integration, Open Systems, Platform, Standards, Systems Integration

Computer   See Mainframe and Minicomputer, Portable Computer, Supercomputer

Computer-Aided Design/Computer-Aided Manufacturing (CAD/CAM)   High-performance computer-aided design (CAD) workstations enable designers to manipulate parts diagrams, simulate operations, infer complete designs from a few specifications, and draw on libraries of designs. In sum, they speed up the design process.

Computer-aided manufacturing (CAM) encompasses an extensive variety of systems designed to facilitate manufacturing, including numerical control, robotics, materials requirement planning, and process control.

CAD/CAM is not just about designing cars or machines. Frito-Lay used it to solve the problem of potato chips getting broken or crushed, and then being unsellable by stores. J.C. Penney designs blouses by CAD/CAM.

CAD/CAM systems can be used to link design and manufacturing. In some firms, CAD designs can be sent directly through telecommunications links to the computer-controlled machines that make the parts.

The extremely fast and powerful workstations responsible for streamlining design and manufacturing look much like personal computers, but they outperform many of today's mid-range host computers in terms of raw speed of computation.

See also: Computer-Integrated Manufacturing, Workstation

Computer-Aided Software Engineering (CASE)   Computer-Aided Software Engineering (CASE) is the use of computer technology to help improve application systems development. CASE consists of a set of workstation-based software tools designed to support application developers: data dictionaries to store and validate definitions of items used in programs and record how and where they are used and calculated; diagnostic tools to check for inconsistencies and redundancy; diagrammatic representations of system designs that can be created quickly and kept up to date and reused in other applications. Developers can design report formats and screen displays at the workstation and when any part of the design is changed, the relevant documents and displays are updated automatically. A few CASE tools generate program code directly from design specifications. Blue Cross/Blue Shield of North Carolina is reported to have built a major system in six months, with CASE tools generating more than 90 percent of the code and programmers custom developing the rest.

CASE tools embody particular development and project management styles or methodologies based on "structured" methods and graphical representations of information and procedures. There are many gaps in existing tools and many competing products, and using them involves learning new ways of operating. Furthermore, implementing CASE is expensive. A leading consultant estimates the five-year cost for introducing CASE tools into an organization with 150 systems professionals at $3.2 million. The initial investment, including hardware, software, and training, is $1.5 million, and annual maintenance costs are $0.35 million. The consultant estimates that to justify such expense, the average productivity gain needs to be 25 percent by the fifth year, since productivity may actually drop in the early years as staff adapt to the new tools.

Business managers need to view CASE as an investment in R&D and organizational development, give proposals a sympathetic hearing, and be skeptical of grandiose promises.

See also: Application Software and Application Development, Programming, Maintenance, Software, Systems Life Cycle, Testing

The tool that will completely solve the problems of software system design, development, and maintenance is not yet here and may never be. Many IT professionals see CASE as an important step forward; many are very disappointed with its progress. They all see software productivity as a fundamental constraint on firms' ability to exploit information technology.

Computer-Integrated Manufacturing (CIM)   Computer-integrated manufacturing involves organization as much as technology.

It refers to the use of IT to streamline manufacturing processes from purchasing and accounting to scheduling, production, and distribution. The logic of CIM is that the systems that control these processes should be able to exchange information with one another directly. Thus a purchase order should automatically update the scheduling system and the production processes should trigger reordering of parts.

This integration of technical processes is also an integration of business and work processes. Implementing CIM involves analyzing, rethinking, and planning each manufacturing process. It also entails overcoming the many incompatibilities between financial and accounting and engineering and manufacturing systems, which have evolved on largely separate hardware and software tracks. Leading computer vendors tend to be strong in one area or the other, but rarely both.

Time-based competition and total quality management have become the main shapers in industry after industry. The leaders in using CIM have cut time by factors of over half. Atlas Door, for instance, has moved to profit leadership in its industry by being able to fulfill a customized order in 3–4 weeks, versus the industry average of 12–15.

Business integration entails rethinking operations designed around separate organizational functions and, in many instances, asking if they are really needed. Ford Motor Company, for example, examined the use of electronic data interchange links to streamline invoicing. As a result, it would be able to reduce its invoicing staff from 500 to 400 people. Further analysis led Ford to entirely eliminate invoices, because the existing EDI systems contained all the relevant data. They cut the staff from 500 down to 100. This "business process reengineering" to use a current term, adopts the view that the best way to automate something is to stop doing it.

Increasingly, companies are reporting that the implementation of computer-integrated manufacturing is much more difficult organizationally than technically. Because CIM redefines skill needs, reporting relationships, information flows, and management, making it work often demands a substantial commitment to education, the development of new incentives, a much more open management style, and a genuine culture of teamwork.

The technology employed in computer-integrated manufacturing extends over the full range of IT, and systems are more distributed than those in banking or airlines. Whereas the latter tend to develop large central systems organized around a key data resource (the reservation data base in airlines and the customer account data base in banking), manufacturing relies on plant and departmental systems located at the site of operations.

Studies of major CIM projects have revealed that the need to integrate what has been termed "islands of information" is frequently the greatest impediment to progress. Firms that lack an overall architecture must first rationalize existing systems and then adopt technology standards that maximize the likelihood of being able to pull existing systems together and ensure that new ones are compatible. The process is a long one.

See also: Computer-Aided Design/Computer-Aided Manufacturing

Computerized Reservation Systems (CRS)   Computerized reservation systems, initially developed by just a few major airlines, constitute the first use of IT that radically altered the dynamics of competition in an entire industry. Prior to airline deregulation, CRSs were viewed as an operational tool — an automated approach to tracking and allocating seat availability — with no apparent competitive relevance. Since deregulation, CRSs have become the core of sales and distribution strategies and yield management for most airlines. (Yield management is the management of on-line pricing and profit — the fine-tuning of discounts to ensure that when a plane takes off it carries the maximum operating profit, the "yield.")

Ownership of a CRS has strongly influenced relative competitive positioning, mergers and acquisitions, marketing options, and pricing. The acknowledged leader in the industry, American Airlines, has turned its CRS, called Sabre, into a multi-use platform that cross-links applications other airlines have built on separate technology bases.

CRSs demonstrate the competitive advantage of occupancy for the early leaders and the ability to add new services to an existing electronic delivery base. By getting there first with good enough systems, American (with Sabre) and United (with Apollo) have been able to fend off competitors for nearly a decade. They have used these infrastructures as the base for alliances (Apollo with Loews hotels and an international CRS consortium called Galileo; Sabre with Hilton, Marriott, and another CRS consortium called Amadeus) and for creating integrated business services (by providing, for example, a single point of contact for airline tickets, hotel bookings, car rental reservations, rail tickets, theater bookings, insurance, and more).

Each of the U.S. and international CRSs has a different technical design philosophy, which has had major business impacts. Sabre, the most centralized and integrated system, allowed American to cross-link its reservation, hubbing, yield management, and frequent flyer programs while the other airlines were building separate bases for each. This afforded American a major competitive advantage throughout the 1980s.

Just about every major alliance, acquisition, and antitrust action in the U.S. and international airline business in the late 1980s centered around ownership of or access to a CRS.

American is currently trying to relieve Sabre's heavy dependence on centralized processing (the overloaded central system failed several times during peak travel periods in 1989 and 1990) by distributing functions to workstations. Covia (the United Airline's IT subsidiary that operates Apollo), driven in part by the Apollo system's inability to keep up with travel agent demand during the early 1980s, had earlier turned to distributed systems and then to "cooperative processing," a move that has given the company an advantage in flexibility in development and operations.

The most important lesson to be learned from the evolution of CRS relates to the importance of senior business management involvement in IT planning. Top management at American Airlines and British Airways, the companies that most violently disrupted the industry status quo, viewed IT as much its responsibility as any other key resource. Other well-run and well-known airlines treated IT as operational overhead, to their continuing competitive cost.

See also: *Cooperative Processing, Distributed Systems, Platform*

Connectivity   It is helpful to think of telecommunications in terms of two questions: "Can we send and receive information between these two locations/devices/business services?" and "Can the transmitted information be interpreted and processed?" The first question relates to connectivity, the second to integration.

Just as telephone companies have made it easy to connect most of the world's telephone systems through direct dial, telecommunications managers and providers have succeeded in interconnecting many of the transmission facilities companies have in place. But just as telephone companies do not provide language lessons to subscribers, telecommunications technicians do not, in general, deal with the many difficulties of sharing different types of information in business applications. In effect, they deal with the problem of how to direct dial Frankfurt from New York, not with the problem of conversing if the communicating parties do not speak the same language.

In terms of IT standards and architectures, the link to Frankfurt corresponds to the lower levels of communication effected by physical and electrical connections and interfaces. These are far easier to define and implement than higher-level standards and architectures for the format and content of business procedures and messages. The 1990s have seen explosive growth in the variety of equipment that provides connectivity across networks, including bridges, routers, gateways, and switches.

Connectivity across different networks, equipment, and services is the core of telecommunications but just a small part of communication.

Managers must recognize that connectivity is not integration, but is a necessary precondition for it. Telecommunications specialists typically focus only on the standards and tools needed to ensure connectivity; the standards and tools needed to increase integration generally lie outside their experience base.

See also: Architecture, Bridges, Routers, and Gateways, Cables, Plugs, and Sockets, Compatibility, Integration, Network, Platform, Standards

Consultative Committee for International Telephony and Telegraphy (CCITT)

The Consultative Committee for International Telephony and Telegraphy (CCITT), part of the International Telecommunications Union headquartered in Switzerland, has been the most influential standard-setting organization in the area of international telecommunications. Its 150 member countries represent the major national telecommunications providers. CCITT standards often take more than a decade to fully define and implement, but once established carry immense weight in the marketplace. The rapid pace of technical change makes such organizations as CCITT less central in the standard-setting process, with key users and vendors playing a more active role and many innovative products becoming de facto standards.

CCITT has been the main standard-setting committee for telecommunications that relate to telephones and public data networks. It represents the supply, rather than demand, side of telecommunications.

See also: International Telecommunications, Standards, Telecommunications

Cooperative Processing

Cooperative processing, one of the newest terms in the IT professional's vocabulary and potentially one of the most important, extends the ideas of distributed systems and the client/server model of computing, to which it is closely related. All three aim at exploiting the relative capabilities of local distributed devices, software, and data bases, and central and shared services such as corporate data bases.

In cooperative processing, work is distributed among client workstations that access servers or other workstations for applications that work together cooperatively. For example, a workstation may initiate a transaction for a customer order that requires software that resides on two different servers and data that reside on a third. All the necessary linkages are established in the act of initiating the relevant transaction; the data-base management systems and the requisite applications work together as needed, entirely transparent to the user, who sees only the results. The workstation drives the processing, making it appear to the user as if all the services needed are in the workstation.

Consider the example of a travel agent making airline, hotel, and car rental reservations for a client. With on-line processing, each activity is handled by a separate reservation system, which can make the process time-consuming, particularly if an availability problem in one system necessitates reaccessing one of the other systems. An intelligent reservation workstation that manages the dialing and automatically accesses each system in response to the agent's selection speeds the process but does nothing about the individual reservation systems' lack of knowledge of one another. Distributing functions to workstations eases the strain on the central reservation mainframe and, by allowing the workstation to store master data for all three reservation systems, enables the travel agent to move among the three systems more easily.

With cooperative processing, the individual systems know about one another and can exchange information automatically. When a change in a passenger's departure date is noted, the three systems cooperatively produce a new set of reservations. With cooperative processing, the agent is no longer handling three separate reservation systems, but managing travel relationships.

Cooperative processing involves complex telecommunications

GE Capital Fleet Services has used cooperative processing to transform service and operations in a complex business. A senior manager commented in early 1991: "The things I'm telling you now I wouldn't have mentioned two years ago because it would have given our competitors wind of what we were doing....by the time they get the system up and running, we're going to be two years further off than that."

networking functions that are the basis for cross-linking separate transactions, hence for creating new, cross-linked business services such as travel relationship management, cross-product financial services and profiles, and so forth. It thus relies on a high degree of integration of the relevant software and telecommunications components of the IT base.

The evolution of modern business computing was initially toward greater distribution of functions, later toward exploiting low cost and powerful workstations, and, most recently, toward building intelligence into the software applications themselves. Client/server and cooperative processing demand an integrated architecture. Only senior business managers can ensure that relevant IT infrastructures and standards are seen as a long-term competitive issue, and not sidetracked by short-term priorities and local business unit needs that push away from integration.

See also: Architecture, Client/Server Model, Computerized Reservation System, Distributed Systems, Network, Platform

Costs of IT   The costs of information technology are paradoxical. On one hand, the price of hardware drops 20–30 percent per year. On the other, the historical rate of growth of information systems budgets over the past three decades has been 15 percent per year. Business executives frequently see IS expenditures as being out of control.

Companies' accounting systems rarely track the real costs of information technology, most of which are hidden. A useful rule of thumb is that the visible price of any IT investment is only 20–25 percent of the full cost. A $5,000 stand-alone personal computer, for instance, becomes a capital investment of $25,000 when the costs of telecommunications, remote data storage, and technical support are added. Every dollar spent on systems development typically generates a follow-on annual cost of forty cents for maintenance of the system and twenty cents for operations. Thus a million-dollar expenditure on systems development ties up four million of capital for the next five years.

Education is a major hidden cost in systems development, especially for systems that change the nature of work rather than merely automate an existing activity. Typically, it amounts to 20 percent of a project budget. Though it is rarely included in the budget, firms typically have to ante up anyway when they discover that effective use of the system demands investment in education.

The hidden and follow-on costs of IT are often overlooked by both business and information systems managers, largely because accounting systems were designed to treat IT as an overhead expense. But information technology has become a capital investment; indeed, it amounts to half the incremental capital expenditures of many large firms. Any firm that does not know its real IT costs, especially hidden and compounded follow-on costs, has no basis for making rational decisions, because the business justification ignores many life cycle costs, hidden costs, and organizational costs.

See also: Application Software and Application Development, Backup and Recovery, Bandwidth, Bridges, Routers, and Gateways, Bug, Business Television, Cables, Plugs, and Sockets, Central Processing Unit, Chargeout and Allocation, Chip, Disk Storage, End-User Computing, Fiber Optics, Forecasting IT Trends, Image Technology, Maintenance, Network Management, Outsourcing, Programming, Prototyping, Security, Testing

Most of the costs of IT are hidden. A reliable rule of thumb is to assume that the price tag is just 20 percent of the full cost.

CPU   see Central Processing Unit

CRS   see Computerized Reservation System

Data   Data are numbers, text, graphics, images, and voice stored in a form that can be processed by a computer. Historically, the term has been used by information systems professionals to describe the numeric and alphabetic contents of computer files and data bases that constituted the bulk of business data processing. A major thrust in telecommunications innovations has been to integrate these varied forms of information; today, any information that is coded digitally can be processed as if it were a single medium. Thus telephone calls, photographs, video frames and electronic transactions have all become "data." (The term "multimedia" is replacing "data" in IT-speak.)

Many commentators on the effective use of IT distinguish "data" from "information," the latter being the meaningful interpretation of the former. The world is awash in data (many older management information systems are little more than bureaucratic aggregations of accounting system data). Useful information is much less plentiful. With Information Services professionals today paying more attention to how to provide information with relevance and meaning, traditional reporting systems are being supplanted by management alerting systems. These collect and store data from core on-line business transaction systems in data bases managed by powerful data base management systems that make it accessible to decision support and executive information systems and other software tools designed to provide relevant information to those who need it, in the form they need it, when they need it.

Managers have too much data and not enough information.

As the use of information becomes an ever more important business tool, competitive advantage accrues to the firm with an IT platform that allows information to be captured, combined, organized, moved, and displayed across locations, levels of staff and managers, and functional areas.

See also: Data-Base Management Systems, Data Communications

Data-Base Management Systems (DBMS) Many different business applications use the same data. For example, the same customer name and address records are used by a bank in its ATM, customer statement, and internal statement and reporting systems. Originally, such records were duplicated and stored in separate files for each application and changes had to be propagated through all the individual systems. Inconsistency was commonplace; redundancy and duplication were enormous.

Data-base management systems (DBMS) function as libraries that make the same information accessible to multiple applications. With a DBMS, a customer's name and address information, for example, need be entered only once and subsequent changes made in only one place. Audit, security, definitions of formats, error-checking, and so forth are handled by the data-base management system.

The breakthrough in DBMS is the "relational" data base (RDBMS), which organizes data in a way that maximizes the variety of ways it can be combined, or "related." This enables an RDBMS to respond to queries such as "Find all employees in the salary range X to Y who have not been promoted in the last five years, indicate their departments and evaluation scores, and identify the evaluators." Because translating such an inquiry and locating the data entail heavy computer overhead, RDBMS technology is not yet suitable for high-volume transaction processing.

A further evolution of RDBMS, still in an early stage of development, is the "distributed relational data-base management system" (DRDBMS), which permits information residing in data bases in different locations to be cross-referenced, updated, and accessed from all locations as if it were in a single, centralized data base.

The major competing RDBMSs are DB2 (an IBM product) and Oracle. The latter's main selling point is the number of different operating systems it runs under. Implementing DB2, Oracle, and other such systems is both organizationally complex, involving procedures for inventorying existing data resources, eliminating duplication, and ensuring consistent formats and definitions of information. It is technically complex in terms of designing the data base structures, ensuring that the needed cross-references between items can be reliably made, and fine-tuning the systems to achieve an acceptable level of efficiency and adequate response time.

To be a true corporate business resource, information must be managed with the same degree of discipline as a firm's budgeting and accounting systems. Indeed, data management may be thought of as a form of information accounting.

Creating a companywide information resource is not the same as creating a universal corporate data base, which is both organizationally and technically impractical. Because just getting agreement on definitions of data items sometimes takes years, efforts to build universal data bases have cost many large companies tens and even hundreds of millions of dollars and have met with little success. A more sensible approach seems to be to evolve sets of key data bases and in the process clean up inaccurate data, generate consistent definitions, install new and reliable procedures, and extend the relevant RDBMS technology across more business functions.

See also: Application Software and Application Development, Data, Platform, Relational Data Base, Systems Integration.

When the Royal Bank of Canada does a mail promotion for a new product, it typically gets a 40 percent response rate versus 2–4 percent for other banks. This is because it has a data base that cross-references information about individual customers in terms of demographics, the products they use and don't use, and their history of transactions. Several credit card providers, by contrast, regularly send junk mail to their own card holders offering them the same card they already have.

Data Center   Traditionally, the corporate data center, the "computer room" as it was called, was a well-guarded facility that housed a firm's mainframe computers, banks of disk and tape drives, and a complement of printers. Mainframes were the dominant form of computing because they offered economies of scale; for twice the price, a company could get four or more times the power. Today, with economies of distribution prevailing over scale, data centers are becoming home to physically smaller mainframe/host computers and greater concentrations of telecommunications devices.

A bias toward personal computers, departmental systems, and distributed computing has led many to argue that corporate data centers are obsolete. Cost per unit is far lower for small, departmental machines, and decentralized IT affords each business unit the autonomy, flexibility, and responsiveness it needs to effectively support its business priorities. Yet many firms, finding that personal computers and other components of the decentralized IT resource are generating new demands for high-performance systems to manage ever-growing data resources, are consolidating multiple smaller data centers. The resulting "mega" data centers also handle coordination of the networks that link corporate data stores with decentralized users. With sales of large computers rivaling the growth of small computer sales, it seems premature to compose a dirge for the mainframe.

See also: Architecture, Chief Information Officer, Hardware, Network Management, Platform, Switch, Terminal

One extreme view of data centers sees them as outdated Kremlins. The other extreme sees them as the equivalent of the Strategic War Rooms of spy films, coordinating a wide range of operations, equipment, and communications vital to the business. Both stereotypes are accurate; the differences are not so much ones of technology as of IS attitude—control versus coordination and business support.

Data Communications   Data communications refers to the transmission of computer-generated information. The term has traditionally been contrasted with voice communications. The world's telephone systems, built to carry voice, are now being redesigned to handle data and, increasingly, data and voice together. Data communication relies on digital transmission, the sending of coded data in rapid pulses. Telephone systems have traditionally relied on analog transmission, in which the sound waves produced by speech are converted into a continuously varying electrical signal. Many of the advances in the technology of telecommunications depend on digital transmission.

Although telephone conversations continue to constitute the

dominant use of telecommunications, the rate of growth of data communications far exceeds that of voice communications. Little by little, voice communications are becoming a subset of data communications, instead of the other way around.

See also: Data, Digital, Transmission

If a mysterious threat stopped all data communications from operating, here are just a few impacts on everyday life: no credit card authorizations, no getting cash from ATMs, no airplane reservations, no insurance application processing, and no Federal Express pickups or deliveries. Data communications are a core business resource, not a technical one.

Data Encryption Standard (DES)   See Encryption

DBMS   See Data-Base Management Systems

Decision Support System (DSS)   A decision support system (DSS) is an information system or analytic model designed to help managers and professionals be more effective in their decision making. A DSS is typically realized in personal computer software that accesses data bases organizationwide. It is not a specific technology, but an emphasis on exploiting available and accessible technologies to support managers, especially in ad hoc analysis and planning.

Decision support systems grew out of management science as much as out of information systems. "Support" emphasizes the focus of these systems on enhancing, rather than replacing, managers' judgment. Early DSSs developed in the mid-1970s included models designed to help product and brand managers plan advertising, promotion, and pricing mixes and financial planners to explore *what if?* scenarios. More recently, the term has been applied to just about any hands-on managerial use of personal computers. The most effective DSSs combine access to remote data bases with analytic models and tools.

Designers of DSSs aim at providing systems that emphasize both usability and usefulness. Usability refers to a system's exploitation of convenient, flexible, and responsive software, including spreadsheets, data-base query languages, and graphical presentation tools. Usefulness refers to a system's contribution to managers' understanding of how complex decision tasks can benefit from the combination of computer power, analytic methods, and managerial judgment.

The term DSS is now so vague as to be indistinguishable from "executive information system" (EIS), "end-user computing," "expert system" and even "personal computing." The real significance of decision support lies not in specific software or personal computers but in what it means to help managers "improve" the effectiveness of their decision making.

See also: *Artificial Intelligence, End-User Computing, Executive Information System, Expert System, User Interface*

DES (Data Encryption Standard)   See Encryption

Desktop Publishing
Desktop publishing is an extension of word processing. It combines sophisticated word processing and graphics software that can incorporate typesetting fonts, color illustration, and even scanned-in photographic images with high-resolution laser printers to make it possible to compose page layouts and generate camera-ready copy in the office.

Organizations are increasingly using desktop publishing to speed production and reduce costs in the creation of reports, in-house magazines, brochures, and the like. The quality of desktop publishing is now so high that a magazine like *Personal Publishing* is entirely produced through it, matching in every way the quality and appearance of any periodical at the newsstand.

See also: *Personal Computer, Word Processing, WYSIWYG*

Development
See Application Software and Application Development

Digital
The entire field of information technology is built on an astonishingly simple base: the ability to represent all types of information as a combination of representations of two conditions — the presence or absence of an electrical signal. These elements, termed *bits,* are represented as ones and zeros, just as the Morse Code uses dots and dashes to indicate letters and numbers. Complex electronic circuits can transmit these digital signals as pulses at rates of millions and even billions per second. The streams of discrete bits can be stored, compressed, checked for errors, and routed efficiently, with dramatic improvements in accuracy, reliability, and speed. The 0–1 digital base,

The logic of decision support is that the combination of managerial judgment, intuition, and experience and computer analysis, data access, display, and calculation will result in more effective and creative decision making than either a manager or a computer could achieve.

used to signal on-off, true-false, yes-no conditions, allows logic circuits to be built to handle calculations quickly.

It is helpful to contrast digital representation, processing, and communication of information with the analog techniques that have long been employed in telephone communication. A telephone creates, in the form of a continuously varying electrical signal, an "analog" of the sound waves generated by the human voice. This analog signal can be converted to a digital signal by sampling it at a sufficient number of points to enable it to be reconstructed at the other end and coding the samples as combinations of bits, which can then be transmitted as pulses. The difference between digital transmission of discrete bits and analog transmission of a continuously varying signal has been likened to the difference between a staccato burst of machine gun fire and a wailing siren of varying intensity.

The managerial relevance of the distinction between analog and digital is that the communication of information — via all media, including telephone, radio, and television — is shifting to digital transmission. This opens a wide range of new communication options within organizations and among customers, suppliers, and partners, albeit often at considerable cost in terms of investment and potential disruption associated with replacing old systems with a new set of infrastructures.

So recent is the digital communication revolution that we can only guess what innovations it might stimulate. As digital transmission speeds increase, more and different kinds of information can be moved onto corporate networks. To code a black-and-white photograph digital form for example, requires about 100,000 bits. To transmit that volume of data would take minutes over analog circuits but less than two seconds over a typical digital link. To take advantage of the innovations spawned by digital transmission, whatever they might be, firms must renew their information infrastructures.

See also: Bits and Bytes, Data, Telecommunications, Transmission

Disk Storage   Disks provide an economical means to store the massive amounts of data accumulated and generated by point-of-sale, on-line customer service, computer-integrated manufacturing, and computerized reservation systems, automated teller machines, and other core IT business applications. These high-density storage devices pack billions of bits of data in a single unit, making it practical for businesses to keep large volumes of information accessible on-line to all the computers in the corporate network.

Personal computer users are familiar with floppy disks (an off-line storage medium) and hard disks (an on-line storage medium). (On-line means that the disk is directly accessible, off-line that it must first be inserted into a disk drive.)

Although relative costs of disk and memory vary widely, a rough approximation of the levels of expenditure for a large firm can be derived from the ratio of 4 gigabytes of disk storage (4 billion bytes) to one mip (millions of instructions per second) of processing power. Each mainframe mip costs about $100,000, each gigabyte of storage about $250,000, yielding a hardware-to-disk storage ratio of 1:10 — $100,000 for memory and $1 million for disk. (These figures were derived from a study conducted by the Gartner Group; although the ratio will vary by firm, the figures suggest the extent to which on-line storage is increasingly a major investment.) For a company with 100 mips of processing power, this translates to $30 million in mainframe computers and $300 million in disk storage (if all the data are to be stored on-line). The mainframe computer does little computing in this context; it primarily manages a gigantic on-line disk library.

The difference between the speed of computer hardware, which processes information in microseconds, or millionths of a second, and disks that provide access to information in milliseconds, or thousandths of a second, is sufficient to make disk input/output frequently a bottleneck in on-line processing systems. A high-performance disk can access and transfer information in under 10 milliseconds. In an on-line business system that handles 500 transactions per second, adding just 3 milliseconds to each transaction will create traffic jams. Disks are inherently slower than chips because they involve moving parts. Much of current innovation in the IT field is in the area of disk storage and management. Among the newer types of storage devices are erasable optical disks, which have far higher retrieval speeds and storage capacity than conventional disks.

See also: Compact Disc-Read Only Memory, Floppy Disk, Hardware, Image Technology

Beware the mainframe bigot who sees no alternative to central iron. Beware the personal computer bigot who sees no value in centralized, shared resources. Beware the local area network bigot who ignores the complexity of interconnecting independent departmental systems.

Distributed Systems   Distributed systems link central "host" computers with decentralized workstations and personal computers for purposes of distributing the processing workload. This contrasts with the pre-personal computer (or pre-intelligent workstation) era in which all processing was done by the host computer, which users accessed via "dumb" terminals.

A number of industries have distributed data and functions previously maintained and performed on central computers to workstations and minicomputers. Airlines' computerized reservation systems are increasingly distributed; travel agency workstations validate dates and airports specified by agents prior to sending the information to the host computer, format information locally into easy-to-read reports, and store profiles of client seat preferences, frequent flyer numbers, addresses, and so forth.

With distribution of functions from mainframes to workstations a nearly universal trend in information technology and decentralized workstations increasingly serving as access points to services, telecommunications networks have become the backbone of the corporate IT resource. Decisions about the use of mainframe, mini-, and microcomputers must today be made with attention to trade-offs among telecommunications and computing costs, power, resource sharing, security, ease of operation, support, and specialized technical requirements, among other factors.

See also: Architecture, Client/Server Model, Cooperative Processing, End-User Computing, Network, Platform

DSS   See Decision Support System

Dumb Terminal   See Terminal

EDI   See Electronic Data Interchange

EDIFACT   EDIFACT is the principal international standard for electronic data interchange. It is sponsored by the United Nations. The cost of paperwork involved in international trade transactions, such as shipping and insurance, is estimated to amount to approximately 7 percent of the cost of the goods involved. EDIFACT establishes the basis for handling these transactions electronically, which would save both time and money and reduce the volume of errors. EDIFACT is closely related to the main U.S. standard for EDI, called X12.

See also: Electronic Data Interchange, Standards

EFTPOS   see Electronic Funds Transfer at Point Of Sale

EIS   See Executive Information System

Electronic Data Interchange (EDI)   Electronic data interchange (EDI) eliminates intermediate steps in processes that rely on the transmission of paper-based instructions and documents by performing them electronically, computer-to-computer. EDI is becoming the norm in intercompany transactions, particularly in ordering, distribution, and payables and receivables.

Consider the following examples of benefits reported by companies that have implemented EDI. The 40-member Petroleum Industry Data Exchange used EDI to eliminate "joint interest billing" documents, which often amounted to thousands of pages that were created, copied, and mailed by partners in a producing well, enabling one firm to reduce its staff by 37 percent. Westinghouse used EDI to streamline the procurement process for a customer, Portland General Electric, reducing elapsed time from order to delivery from 15 days to one-half day and processing costs from $90 to $10. Levi-Strauss's Levilink EDI enabled one customer to reduce the replenishment cycle for its chain of 60 stores from 14 to 3 days and order delivery time from 9 to 3 days and to entirely eliminate its regional warehouses. Linking 100 customers to its purchasing and payments systems via EDI has saved R.J. Reynolds between $5 and $10 million in costs of labor, inventory, and lead times and led the firm to offer a 5 percent discount to customers that pay via EDI. Finally, the Port of Rotterdam's INTIS cargo clearing system clears goods on average in 15 minutes, compared to the previous 2 days, and has substantially reduced the nearly 50 percent return of export order documents for errors.

Such quantifiable economic and less "hard" organizational ben-

Other countries are well ahead of the United States in implementing electronic data interchange as an explicit part of economic policy. In Singapore, Hong Kong, and Rotterdam EDI is used to process government documents and clear goods through customs in 10–15 minutes versus the typical 2–3 days.

efits, together with the growing trend among firms to require it of their suppliers, make EDI one of the major emerging competitive uses of IT for the 1990s. Firms that have implemented EDI effectively have been able to streamline operations, shrink administration, reduce errors and delays, and generally improve service.

Companies with market dominance are increasingly requiring suppliers to link to their EDI systems and refusing to deal with those that refuse or cannot. The chairman of Sears for example, informed the firm's suppliers by letter in mid-1990 that they would have to link to its EDI systems. To smooth the transition, Sears offered training and free software. General Motors has had such a requirement in place for several years. As more companies move in this direction, EDI becomes a competitive necessity for small as well as large firms.

The technical base for EDI is relatively simple. Rather than require that firms use the same document formats, it exploits standards that provide for local translation of incoming and outgoing messages into appropriate formats. The relevant standards include X12, the closely related international EDIFACT, and X.400 (a more general, less comprehensive standard for simple electronic messages).

To be able to use the standards effectively, EDI partners must agree on terminology — for example, that "weight" will mean "gross weight," not "net weight," or that "DM" will refer to "Deutschmark." One reason that many companies are adopting EDIFACT is that it provides dictionaries of agreed-on standard terms for many aspects of international trade. More broadly, industry groups are cooperating on the development of trading standards. Because all parties concerned are looking to reach a mutually beneficial agreement, the standard-setting process is proceeding more rapidly in EDI than in other areas of IT.

As is often the case in IT, the most complex aspects of EDI are organizational rather than technical. EDI requires that firms rethink business processes, not just try to make the paper chains faster and existing bureaucratic procedures more efficient. Any major IT innovation that is also an innovation in work must get by issues of standards, architecture, incompatibility, organizational change and learning, and inappropriate business justification — the old refrain of reasons for implementation failures. But impediments to implementation not-

It is possible, though dumb, to run a business without using telephones. In more and more industries, it is just as dumb not to use EDI.

withstanding, the benefits of EDI are so great that it is safe to predict that it will be one of the fastest growing and most pervasive applications of IT in the early 1990s.

See also: Architecture, Distributed Systems, EDIFACT, Network, Platform, Standards

Electronic Funds Transfer at Point of Sale (EFTPOS)

Electronic funds transfer at point of sale (EFTPOS) is the combination of electronic banking with point-of-sale retailing. The business logic is that of a cash transaction: payment is made at time of purchase. For example, you present your ATM card when you buy goods, and the EFTPOS system immediately debits your bank account.

But business logic may not match consumer emotion. EFTPOS eliminates float, the time between the writing of a check and the debiting of a bank account. With a debit card, funds leave the bank account at the instant of purchase, an event customers accustomed to credit cards may find unsettling. Consumers have yet to see sufficient benefit from debit cards to compensate for the loss of three to five days of float. Ninety-five percent of the approximately 2 million POS terminals in use in the United States handle credit card or check payment authorizations. Debit card payments have barely grown in the past decade.

Mobil Oil's EFTPOS pilot, by eliminating paperwork and delays in handling credit cards, checks, and "real" money, enabled the company to offer service stations and consumers each a 4-cents-per-gallon reduction in price and still save money. Whether this will prove to be sufficient incentive to consumers remains to be seen.

See also: Automated Teller Machines, On-Line Transaction Processing, Point of Sale, Smart Card

Electronic Mail

Electronic mail enables people to send messages to one another without having to make direct contact or know one another's location. An electronic mail service maintains a directory of subscribers, for whom it stores messages on disk. When a subscriber accesses the electronic mail facility, from home, office, or hotel, any waiting messages are delivered.

Electronic mail brings communication to you the user, irrespective of time and place. It eliminates "telephone tag"; it enables you to drop a line to a colleague when a telephone call would be inconvenient; it provides a way to keep in touch casually and unobtrusively with a network of contacts.

Both public and private electronic mail systems exist. Most public services are offered by telecommunications providers, such as AT&T, Compuserve, MCI, and Western Union. Private electronic mail systems are usually accessible only to authorized subscribers — typically, individuals within a firm or organization — and until recently required specific equipment, networks, and software. A number of electronic mail systems that run on local area networks are offered for departmental or other in-house use. The recent and rapid implementation of the X.400 standard has made many previously incompatible electronic mail services interconnectable.

"I am simply amazed by how little I need the telephone now and how many different types of bulletin, newsboards, and data bases I can access through e-mail. I can even send a fax through it. I am appalled, though, by how much electronic junk mail I get."—a senior World Bank executive, commenting on the bank's worldwide electronic mail system that has contributed to Jakarta becoming "The Washington night shift."

Interconnectivity notwithstanding, most electronic mail systems need to be made easier to use. The explosive growth of portable fax, which is relatively inexpensive, simple to use, and convenient, is in stark contrast to the slow growth of electronic mail. Despite its proven benefits and the proliferation of personal computers, which need only a modem to access public electronic mail services, e-mail remains underutilized. Its main users continue to be people who travel a lot, for whom electronic mail is an essential complement to the telephone. This user base is not likely to explode until the use of electronic mail is made more intuitive and simple.

See also: Business Television, Cellular Communication, Mobile Communication, Network, Standards, Videoconferencing

Encryption   Encryption is a technique for ensuring the security of information to be transmitted over a telecommunications line by scrambling it at one end and unscrambling it at the other. Keys for scrambling the information are generated by mathematical algorithms, several of which are said to be so complex that they could not be decoded in the lifetime of the universe. The standard encryption technique is called Data Encryption Standard, or DES.

Mobile telephone conversations that are neither encrypted nor protected by law from eavesdropping are easily tapped by a radio hobbyist. The same is true for many business transactions sent over public telephone lines. Encryption removes this risk by ensuring that data tapped during transmission will be incomprehensible.

See also: Security, Telecommunications, Transmission

End-User Computing   End-user computing refers to uses of IT that are entirely under the control of business units and do not require traditional IT application systems development and operations expertise. This includes general uses of personal computers and many of the software packages that run on them, such as data base management, decision support, executive information, desktop publishing, and word processing systems, electronic spreadsheets, and others.

End-user computing has grown to such an extent that in many large firms more than 50 percent of computing expenditures now fall outside the Information Services department's budget. Accounting systems rarely identify the full cost of IT and many companies significantly underestimate how much they spend on end-user computing. Often, companies generate elaborate and formal business-justification procedures for the visible, central IT function, while handling end-user computing on a laissez-faire basis. Companies that sensibly require detailed justification for a $2 million mainframe purchase often do not accord the same attention to one thousand purchases of personal computers at $3,500 each. End-user computing is as much a capital commitment as central Information Systems and should receive as sophisticated an economic analysis.

Many IS groups view end-user computing as both a priority and a problem. It is a business priority that they must and generally want to support, especially in terms of technical advice and guidance in choosing standards, equipment, and software. It is a problem in that end-user facilities are increasingly interdependent and need to mesh with the corporate architecture, necessitating cross-functional and cross-locational telecommunications links and access to corporate data resources. Defining the role of central IS within a decentralized business and the balance between central coordination and decentralized use is an important issue for IS managers and can be a major source

An Argentinian rival of a Swiss pharmaceutical firm brought out a version of the Swiss company's patented new drug before it was launched in Argentina. The Swiss firm is sure that an employee of the Argentinian telecommunications agency copied key research documents that were sent from Switzerland through an unencrypted transmission link.

Do-it-yourself use of computers, ranges from personal computers to office technology to fourth-generation languages. The term is largely obsolete now, but in the late 1970s end-user computing represented a radical change—and a radical shift of control and influence from central MIS groups to business units.

of tension for business units. Traditionally a systems developer and facilities operator, Information Systems is today called upon to build the infrastructures that will enable business users to get the most value from IT, without compromising the autonomy of business units in the use of their own IT tools.

As end-user computing becomes embedded in the everyday activities of organizations, business units find that they need to develop new capabilities and management processes. Departmental IT resources such as local area networks, data-base management systems, distributed processing, electronic mail, desktop publishing and a wide range of software come with attendant needs for security, auditing, maintenance, and training. End-user computing has clearly become as much of a management challenge as the central IS function.

Education must be a priority to obtain value from end-user computing. Education is not the same as training. One "trains" people in the use of a particular software package, such as a word processing system, usually through short courses that mainly address the mechanics of use. One "educates" people about how to use these tools effectively in their job, evaluate and incorporate new software and uses of software, manage data resources, and ensure security. The product of a training program is a user proficient in an application. The product of an education program is a self-sufficient user.

End-users often underestimate how much they need to know to move beyond simple stand-alone personal computer applications. Departmental systems of intelligent workstations, local area networks, and data-base management software are technically more complex than the data centers of the 1970s. How to provide support and education needed to make these systems operationally effective is a major concern of firms today, and a large and growing, but often hidden, cost.

See also: *Client/Server Model, Cooperative Processing, Decision Support System, Executive Information System*

Ethernet   Ethernet is a local area network standard widely used in large organizations. Ethernet is easy to install, widely implemented in products, and well suited to connecting workstations and departmental computers. Its strength is its simplicity and ease of expansion; its main limitation is its susceptibility to congestion when handling heavy communications traffic. Ethernet is best suited to short, intermittent message traffic.

The evolution of Ethernet highlights the importance of what may seem a trivial consideration to business mangers: cabling. The original Ethernet standard specified coaxial cable (the same cable used to connect a VCR to a television set), which costs about 75 cents per foot. A later version of Ethernet, designated 10Base-T, specifies standard, unshielded twisted pair cable (ordinary telephone wire) which costs 5 cents per foot. Other local area network technologies use entirely different cabling to the extent that even in 1991 many industry groups were drafting standards to help network managers deal with what one expert called "a bewildering array of wire."

Ethernet's principal competitor in the large organization local area network arena is IBM's Token Ring standard. Ethernet and Token Ring local area networks can be interconnected, at a cost, but their design principles and comparative advantages are entirely different. Fiber-optic-based LANs are complementing or replacing both Ethernet and Token Ring. FDDI is the standard here.

See also: Bridges, Routers, and Gateways, Local Area Network, Network, Token Ring, Transmission

Executive Information System (EIS) An executive information system (EIS) delivers, analyzes, and displays on a business manager's workstation information that gives him or her a clearer picture of key trends and events before it is too late to do something about them. The data, typically market figures, financial information, and industry statistics, are culled from both firms' on-line business processing systems and third-party organizations.

Frito-Lay has been particularly effective in transforming traditional, report-based management information systems into executive information systems that empower executives. Frito-Lay's 10,000 sales representatives daily use hand-held computers to access central database information on inventory, prices, promotions, and so forth and to record their sales data. The data are transmitted by telecommunica-

If you as a business manager could come into your office in the morning, switch on your personal computer, and immediately get just one screen of information that would tell you if things are under control or there is something you need to either take action on yourself or alert your subordinates to, what would be on that screen? It would not be a summary of last month's sales, but it might be yesterday's sales, or yesterday's production, or yesterday's stockouts, or even yesterday's number of customer complaints.

tions to Frito-Lay's central computers. This activity puts the information system ahead of the accounting system; it enables the company's 32 divisional managers to examine sales figures for every one of the company's product lines in every type of store in their territory as of the time of their query. They can examine top and bottom performers, obtain information about a competitor (pressing a green gremlin displays new information on competitors), check sales for a given product at a particular store, highlight unusual or troubling data, and analyze trends, both short and long term. Senior executives can access status reports by product and/or region via a touch screen menu on their personal computers.

Frito-Lay's EIS is not an application, but an infrastructure that includes point-of-event data capture tools (e.g., hand-held computers, point-of-sale terminals, and internal customer service workstations); communications links across the firm (extending to the distribution centers where sales representatives plug in their hand-helds at the end of each day); a massive data base engine — an enormous, expensive, complex software system running on giant mainframes that coordinates information ranging from the operational data captured by hand-held computers to purchased data obtained from market research firms); and special-purpose software designed to quickly extract, organize, manipulate, and display information in a meaningful form.

Implementation of this infrastructure took more than a decade, and new services are constantly being added to it. Because it would be extremely costly and time-consuming to replicate, it assures Frito-Lay a distinctive competitive edge that will be difficult for other firms to match.

See also: Architecture, Decision Support System, Expert System, Platform

Expert System   An expert system is the codification in software of the knowledge of an expert or experts in a specific domain. Digital Equipment Corporation, for example, developed an expert system called XCON that configures computer systems, a highly complex task that involves many different combinations of cabling, connectors, and components. XCON outperforms humans, not because it possesses superior intelligence, but because it contains so many simple rules that experience shows are relevant to choosing options. Another expert system success is Boeing's Case (connector assembly specification expert) system, which tells workers how to assemble each of appproximately 5,000 multiple electrical connectors for an airplane using more than 500 different types of connector. Previously, workers had to pore over 20,000 pages of manuals to find the right parts and tools. What took workers more than 40 minutes takes Case just five.

Capturing the knowledge to be put into an expert system is usually accomplished by interviewing acknowledged experts. Codification of the knowledge is carried out by "knowledge engineers" using "knowledge representation" techniques. The highly specialized technology and tools of expert systems include expert system "shells," software tools that provide a framework for assembling and using rule-based knowledge.

An expert's knowledge and the rules that govern how to apply it are generally coded in the form of "if…then…else" statements. Consider an experienced travel agent's explanation of how to find the least expensive fare for a passenger who wants to fly from New York to Los Angeles:

"First, I check how many days notice I have. If the passenger is booking more than 60 days ahead, I know I am likely to find a deal. If it's seven days or less, forget it.

"If the journey is around the main holidays, I don't expect to find any low fares. But if it is actually on, say, Thanksgiving or Christmas Day, I can almost guarantee to find one. Why? Because the planes are full the day before Thanksgiving and the day after, but empty on the holiday itself."

Capturing and representing such knowledge is a difficult process; it turns out that the more expert people are, the more they tend to internalize their expertise and the less able they are to articulate it. We use words like "intuition," "gut feel," and "wisdom" to summarize insights that cannot be easily articulated and hence turned into rules for expert systems.

Like so many aspects of IT, expert systems and artificial intelligence were embarrassingly overhyped in the 1980s. Knowledge engineers

"Expert" need not mean "learned and very important person." Experimental early expert systems focused on medical diagnosis. The ones that have been most effective address such tasks as credit card authorization, finding the lowest airline fare, and configuring computer cables.

claimed that they could capture expertise and build systems that would make experts obsolete. They couldn't and didn't.

More realistic expert systems builders recognized the complexity of the design and implementation process, the difficulty of capturing knowledge, of building and testing the system, and of helping people feel comfortable using it. They saw expert systems not in terms of fast or magic payoffs, but as a long-term direction of effort. And they chose problems to which the rule-based approach was well suited.

A 1990 study of expert systems in a variety of companies estimated development costs at from $50,000 for a system to be used by a few individuals to as much as $500,000 for a system that targets complex areas of decision-making.

See also: Artificial Intelligence, Prototyping

When fax machines were expensive, slow, and few in number, there was no, "I'll fax it up to your floor" in the same building, no ordering pizza by fax, no sending a fax to or from a car, and no masses of junk fax jamming up your machine. Effective IT innovations frequently go well beyond just automating the status quo, and their impacts are unpredictable. New tools create new uses.

Facsimile   A facsimile, or fax, machine scans a printed page and converts it to a signal that is transmitted over a telephone line to a receiving fax machine. Fax machines have been in use for decades, but until recently were slow and expensive. Today, low-cost portable fax machines are almost as much an everyday necessity as telephones.

There are four fax standards, termed Groups. The machines used in the 1970s, which took several minutes to transmit a page and had to be connected to machines of the same group, were termed Groups 1 and 2 fax. Today's standard fax machine, which transmits a page in less than a minute, is Group 3 fax.

Group 3 fax machines use analog transmission. Newer, more expensive fax machines use digital transmission, which is much faster. They constitute Group 4 fax. Beyond speed of transmission, digital fax has the advantage of coding a document in a form that can be processed by any other digital device, making it acceptable input to a computer program. This renders fax an integral component in firms' Information Systems platforms.

See also: Digital, Platform, Transmission

FAX   See Facsimile

FDDI   See Fiber Distributed Data Interface (FDDI)

Fiber Distributed Data Interface (FDDI)   Fiber distributed data interface, or FDDI, is a recent standard for fiber optic local area networks (LANs). FDDI-based LANs transmit data at 100 million bits per second, ten times faster than Ethernet-based LANs and six times faster than Token Ring networks, opening up possibilities for many new applications of IT. At this speed, the transmission of large data bases and high-resolution images of documents and video can be supported.

See also: Fiber Optics, Local Area Network, Standards, Transmission

Fiber Optics   Optical fiber, a glass wire thinner than a human hair designed to transmit light, is one of the true wonders of our age. One recent claim holds that a single fiber strand will eventually be able to transmit 2 trillion bits per second; the total transmission of the entire telecommunications industry today, including AT&T, MCI, US Sprint, and the Bell Operating Companies, is only 1 trillion bits per second. At present, typical fiber speeds are in excess of a billion bits a second. The SONET standard operates at 2.5 billion bits per second. An early version of SONET was introduced in Chicago in early 1991.

It will take time for telephone companies in the United States and abroad to replace all existing copper cable with fiber, but the process has begun. Transatlantic telephone capacity doubled with the installation of the 8-fiber strand TAT-8 system. Fiber optic-based local area networks are becoming increasingly common, with the FDDI standard (fiber distributed data interface) providing speeds of 100 million bits per second (contrast this with high-speed, cable-based local area networks, for which the upper limit is currently 16 million bits per second) and wide area fiber optic networks are expected by optimistic commentators before 1993 (and by pessimists before 1996). The principal standard for fiber wide area networks, SONET, is being promoted by AT&T.

Fiber transmission speeds do not translate directly into transaction processing speeds any more than aircraft speeds translate into travel times. Airport congestion and delays, check-in, and road traffic all extend total journey time. Their equivalents in communications are the switches that route traffic onto the backbone network, which are not yet fast enough to take full advantage of fiber speeds.

Apart from speed and cost, fiber optics offers several advantages over cable — among them, reliability and security. Fiber links, unlike cables that transmit electrical signals, cannot be tapped. The vulnerability of fiber is that if the hair-thin strand is cut, transmission ceases. United Airlines, realizing that the fiber strands that carry 100,000 simultaneous transmissions are usually buried only a few feet underground, dispatched a team to post the locations of some of its own fiber cable. Unfortunately, one of the signs was driven through the cable it was to protect, knocking out the airline's reservation system and halting marketing and sales for several hours. A British cable manufacturer had a similar experience; it planted a Christmas tree through the main cable of its head office building. Every large company is vulnerable to such chance interruptions of service. The more of its fiber's capacity a company uses, the more it will need to provide redundancy and backup linkages and establish recovery procedures. The prospect of simultaneously interrupting 100,000 telephone conversations, and the cash flow and customer service of any number of businesses, is daunting, indeed.

The billion-bits-per-second speeds of fiber may seem like a solution looking for a problem. Business communications today largely operate at speeds from 56 to 64 thousand bits per second. What will firms do with the extra capacity fiber affords? First, they will share it, by "multiplexing" many low-speed transmissions onto the fiber. They will also use it to move large data bases between locations electronically. Most important, they will use it for novel video, image, and engineering applications. An example of what fiber might make practical and cost-effective is interactive access from a computer-aided design workstation to a full-color, full-motion, detailed design simulation of car performance running on a supercomputer. To provide the picture quality of a good photograph with the quality of movement on television or film requires a resolution of a megabit of pixels (the tiny dots that make up an image on a monitor display) per frame and a transmission speed of 720 megabits per second. To provide full-color, multiply these requirements by 24 bits per pixel. To ensure full motion

In the spring of 1991, Teleport Chicago began operating the first telecommunications network based on the fiber optics SONET international standard. It can transmit data at up to 2.5 billion bits a second. Fiber-based local area networks transmit at up to 100 million bits a second. These represent a many-hundredfold improvement in less than ten years.

quality, the images must be sent at 30 frames per second (the same speed used in projecting films). Clever tricks of data compression can reduce this to 15 megabits per second. Such an application is utterly impractical with current telecommunications speeds.

See also: Bandwidth, Digital, FDDI, International Telecommunications, Network, Standards, Switch, Telecommunications, Transmission

Floppy Disk   Personal computers, like larger computers, are provided with disk drives that allow users to load programs and data stored on disks into the computer's main memory. Floppy disks take their name from the 5.25 inch bendable diskettes that were used in earlier models of word processors and personal computers. The more common 3.5 inch diskette that is becoming the standard for personal computers, though decidedly not floppy, seems to be stuck with the name. The storage capacity of a 3.5 inch "floppy," which can be double-sided and/or double density, ranges from 720 thousand to 2 million bytes.

See also: Disk Storage, On-Line

Forecasting IT Trends   IT trend estimates are generally wildly optimistic. Attach your own labels to the axes of the following general-purpose graph taken from a 1990 estimate, and you can be a forecaster of the next IT fad.

Variants of this curve appear in many advertisements and reports. Occasionally, they accurately predict acceleration of demand for an IT component. More often, they compress into five years what will take ten to fifteen. Vendor hopes obviously drive many of the most wildly optimistic estimates. In 1983, for example, a well-respected firm forecast 1987 sales for consumer videotex services at $7 billion. Actual sales were well under 10 percent of that. Yet, two years after the disappointing news, the same firm estimated that videotex would grow at 25 percent per year through 1993. It hasn't and won't.

Forecasts of the take-off of new technology and applications generally ignore the social and organizational change needed to make them effective and the long learning curve that keeps old tools and habits in place, especially when they meet existing needs. A more

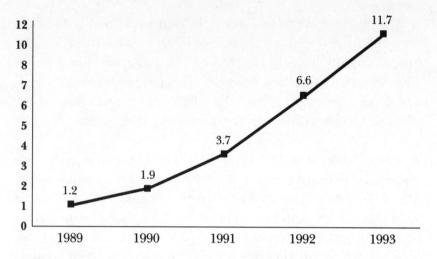

Historically, once an IT innovation reaches a critical mass of users, it grows at a rate of between 10 and 20 percent a year. Until it reaches that take-off point, it is generally impossible to predict its growth. That does not seem to stop vendors and consultants from drawing graphs showing dramatic exponential growth from today's tiny base, even though their last prediction of an $X billion market by 1991 was off by two or even three zeroes.

reliable projection of the acceleration of demand is that old stand-by, the S-curve. The S-curve breaks the introduction of new technology into three distinct stages: initiation, take-off, and maturation.

For stand-alone personal computers (i.e., those without tele-communications capability), a short initiation phase (about 5 years) was followed by a roughly equal period of rapid and steep take-off (personal computer sales exceeded 20 million per year by 1990) and maturation, with slowing sales driven primarily by the replacement market. The curve for videoconferencing, on the other hand, can hardly be called that as it continues to hug the horizontal axis after more than 20 years (although there are hints that it may be moving to the take-off stage).

Premature predictions of the cashless society, paperless office, telecommuting, and the factory of the future were products of overextrapolation from a few early pilots or isolated successes. Managers for whom the future turns out to be like the past are naturally inclined to be skeptical of the next set of claims. It is becoming clear that technology generally moves faster, and organizational and social change much slower, than we predict. It is a rare IT-based innovation that does not involve major rethinking, relearning, trial and error, development of new skills and processes, and an often disruptive shift from old systems and procedures to new ones.

The proven lead time for business and organizational innovations that require major investment in IT infrastructures is seven years, and it is difficult to develop any significant application in less than two years. Even when the hardware and software can be bought off the shelf, the organizational process of piloting, design, implementation, education, and organizational learning cannot be hurried without risk of disaster and fiasco.

The principal source of competitive advantage from IT relates to the time gap between leaders and laggards. A new product or service that is based on a personal computer and a purchased software package can generally be matched fairly quickly by competitors. But with an innovation built on such complex infrastructures as a global telecommunications network or comprehensive relational data-base capability and involving major shifts in organization, learning, and skills, catch up is measured in years.

It is important in assessing any forecast of IT innovation to question the assumptions that underlie it. Managers need to assess likely business, organizational, and social forces that may either slow or speed progress along the curve. Then they must ask, "Is a move that will put us ahead of the pack worth the risk?" "Should we wait and follow?" "How long can we wait before we risk being unable to catch up?"

See also: Chief Information Officer, Cost of IT

Fortran   See Programming

Fourth-Generation Language (4GL)   A fourth-generation language, or 4GL, is a software facility designed to speed up application development, by allowing programmers to use English-like commands and step-by-step procedures that would otherwise have to be specified in detail. Report writers, for example, will automatically generate the code to handle pagination, calculations of totals, and other minor but essential operations for which the programmer would otherwise have to write instructions.

The term "fourth generation" places the language in the context of the history of programming. First-generation programming languages required programmers to work at the level of the machine instruction code, an intensely slow and tedious process. Second- and

A 1991 survey of software productivity found that small, medium, and large firms all identified 4GLs as the tool that most reduced software development and maintenance costs.

third-generation languages put successively more distance between programmers and the computer's native tongue. The "higher-level" third-generation languages most widely used today, such as COBOL, generate many machine code instructions for a single line of "source code" written by a programmer. Fourth-generation languages are a further refinement in using English-like commands to tell a computer what to do. Because of the overhead incurred in translating high-level commands into machine instructions, 4GLs are most effective in speeding the development of smaller systems. They are less efficient for developing large systems and systems designed to handle heavy transaction volumes.

See also: *Application Software and Application Development, Computer-Aided Software Engineering, Programming, Object-Oriented Programming, Software, Systems Life Cycle*

Gateway   See Bridges, Routers, and Gateways

Gigahertz   See Megahertz and Gigahertz

Graphical User Interface   Apple's dual innovation of the electronic mouse and icon-based menu with its Macintosh personal computer transformed user interaction with computers. The Macintosh, or Mac, displays users' options in the form of graphic images, termed icons, to which the user points using a mouse, a palm-sized device attached to the computer, the movement of which corresponds to the movement of a cursor on a screen. The user selects an option by moving the mouse to position the cursor over it and pressing a button on top of, or "clicking," the mouse.

The central principle underlying the design of almost all personal computer and workstation software today is that the system (not the users) should handle complexity, that users should not have to remember what options are available but be presented with them, and that users should be able to point instead of type.

This "graphical-user-interface" approach to using computers underlies most recently introduced, successful IT products targeted at occasional, inexperienced users. Lotus 1-2-3, the personal computer spreadsheet that transformed business use of computers in the mid-1980s, permits a user to move the cursor around the screen to select a column, and Microsoft's Windows 3.0 turns an IBM personal computer running the MS.DOS operating system into a Macintosh look-alike. This design approach to interaction between user and computer has clearly helped to bring what was a technology for specialists into the office, home, and classroom.

See also: *End-User Computing, User, User Friendly, User Interface*

Hand-Held Computer   See Portable Computer

Hardware   Hardware refers broadly to the physical components of information technology, the computers, peripheral devices, such as printers, disks, and scanners, and the cables, switches, and other elements of the telecommunications infrastructure that connect everything together.

Hardware is the engine of computing, chips its key component. The compounded 20–30 percent improvement in price performance of chips translates directly into continuous cost reductions in hardware. The same is not true for software, which remains labor-intensive.

There are two main categories of hardware: processors and peripherals. Processors are computers and telecommunications controllers of varying sizes and types that operate at speeds measured in microseconds and picoseconds (millionths and trillionths of a second, respectively). Peripherals are devices that attach to processors: disk drives, printers, computer monitors, and so forth. They almost invariably include moving parts that limit their speeds to milliseconds (thousandths of a second) and even seconds. As a result, peripheral performance has not kept pace with processor performance. IDC, a leading IT research firm, estimates that between 1980 and 1990 performance of mainframe CPUs improved by a factor of seven, performance of "input/output subsystems" by a factor of less than two.

See also: *Cables, Plugs, and Sockets, Disk Storage, Fiber Optics, Mainframe and Minicomputer, Personal Computer*

If anything, the hardware revolution is just beginning and the astonishing innovations of the 1980s will seem trivial by the mid-1990s. It is unlikely that we will say the same about software; the breakthroughs are yet to come.

Host Computer   "Host" is increasingly being used instead of mainframe or minicomputer to describe a computer that provides services to a range of workstations.

See also: *Client/Server Model, Distributed Systems, Mainframe and Minicomputer, Platform, Workstation*

IBM and IBM-Compatible Computer See Personal Computer

Icon   See User Interface

Image Technology   Image technology refers to the general category of computer applications that convert documents, illustrations, photographs, and other images into data that can be stored, distributed, accessed, and processed by computers and special-purpose workstations. Large-scale image processing systems have only recently become widely available.

Most major companies have at least one large-scale pilot image application under development, and a number of firms have used image technology in core business operations, with significant economic and organizational gains. One of these is USAA, a leading insurance firm that pioneered image processing as part of a long-term business vision of becoming the most responsive firm in the industry, a position it is generally acknowledged to have achieved. Image technology has enabled USAA to bring together in a single electronic folder all the records and documents relevant to a customer, ranging from correspondence to policies to photographs to claims history, and put it at the agent's fingertips when a customer calls.

Another successful user of image technology is Northwest Airlines, which uses it in passenger revenue accounting, the time-consuming and tedious process of examining boxes of used airline tickets to audit inter-airline payments, foreign currency adjustments, accuracy of pricing, and so forth. Previously Northwest was able to deal manually with only 5 percent of the annual 20 million tickets. The image processing system audits 60,000 tickets per day with greater accuracy and produces more timely management information. The system paid for itself in a mere three months.

Empire Blue Cross and Blue Shield reduced the time required to process Medicare claims from seven days to two and cut direct costs by 15 percent using image processing, and American Express, by providing a high-quality image of each transaction on a customer's billing statement, was able to improve the quality and differentiation of its services while reducing billing costs by 25 percent. Phoenix Mutual

Equity Planning Corporation has used the technology to reduce lead time for a mutual fund purchase from 22 days to one and cut staff requirements by 30 percent.

The technology base for companywide image processing comprises several components. A scanner transforms physical images into electronic digitized images, which must then be indexed and compressed. Data-base management software handles the accessing of the indexed images, and a server/controller moves them to and from storage, which is typically magnetic or optical disk or some combination of these, and routes them through the corporate network. High-powered workstations and high-resolution display screens are needed to display and manipulate the images.

These components are all far more expensive than the computers, software, and workstations that handle transactions and data. Even a small departmental system with fewer than a dozen users will cost close to half a million dollars. To commit fully to image processing will cost a large firm from ten to hundreds of millions of dollars.

However costly image processing might be, the potential payoff from successful incursions in the war against the paper mountain can dwarf its expense. Given estimates by Wang that less than 5 percent of company information is stored on computers, and Exxon, which calculated that every document in its head office is copied forty times with fifteen copies being permanently stored in filing cabinets, the business and organizational opportunities that image technology presents are clearly immense. U.S. businesses are estimated to store close to half a trillion documents per year. It is not unusual for many office and administrative staff to spend 20 percent of their work day just trying to locate documents.

The 1980s was the decade of the personal computer. The 1990s is the decade of image technology.

The 1980s was the decade of the personal computer. The 1990s will be the decade of image technology.

See also: *Bar Code, Forecasting Information Technology Trends*

Incompatibility   One might expect that a program that runs on one computer would be able to run on another, that a printer connected to one computer would be connected to another computer, and that data disks ought to be able to be shared between two

Incompatibility is the cause of almost every major problem in information technology. Business managers unwittingly have created much of the incompatibility of multivendor, multitechnology chaos that marks most organizations.

computers. The term incompatibility is used to explain why two components will not work together, which is all too often the case. Differences in hardware design, operating systems, data representation schemes, standards, and protocols make incompatibility the norm in IT. One of the primary goals of developing a corporate IT architecture is to evolve an integrated capability and end the chaos of components and systems that ought to work together but cannot.

The explanation for the widespread incompatibility among systems and components lies in the history of the IT industry. The IT field grew as a result of individual manufacturers developing their own hardware, operating systems, and telecommunications equipment. Specifications for these products were proprietary. There was little cooperation among suppliers and only a few industrywide standards, many of which leading vendors, especially IBM, ignored.

This situation persisted through the 1970s. Little by little, momentum built for standards, primarily in the field of international telecommunications. Today, every major vendor and user recognizes that standards are essential, but the technology changes so quickly that it is difficult to freeze specifications or keep standards current.

Although progress continues to be made toward achieving compatibility among the key elements of the IT infrastructure, there is a massive investment in existing incompatible systems that are too costly to redesign and replace. Resolving these problems is the core of the Information Systems planners' job.

See also: *Architecture, Compatibility, Integration*

Information Technology (IT)   Through the early 1980s, "computers" covered just about the whole field of information processing. Now, "information technology" has become the generally accepted umbrella term for a rapidly expanding range of equipment, applications, services, and basic technologies. They fall into three primary categories: computers, telecommunications, and multimedia data, with literally hundreds of subcategories. Increasingly, the three elements have become interdependent. A "server," for instance, is a computer that is a key element in a client/server environment on a local area network and will manage shared data bases.

See also: *The introduction to this book*

Integrated Services Digital Network (ISDN) Integrated Services Digital Network is the plan for the long-promised transition of the world's telephone systems from analog to digital technology to permit the combined transmission of any and every type of information, including voice, pictures, newspapers, diagrams, and even videoconferencing. Telephone systems today are limited in the amount and type of information they can transmit and receive and the special facilities they can provide. ISDN is a prescription for a telephone system that can deliver any type of information at 10 to 30 times today's speeds and simultaneously handle two entirely different applications on the same line, for example, a telephone call and transaction processing.

ISDN, a 1970s' concept that originated in Europe, now that it is actually being implemented is viewed by some experts and managers as obsolete and superfluous. Many of its design features, which were fairly advanced when they were defined, are already available in a variety of non-ISDN products. The design has not kept pace with newer technologies and newer applications, and there are many variations in implementations of ISDN standards.

It is unclear how effective ISDN will be in the United States. Businesses now have so many choices that they may not benefit from ISDN. Consumers should, but not until the cost of the equipment that replaces the old telephone handset and the charges for monthly use become attractive. European and Asian countries are firmly committed to ISDN, in part because they have a lot of catching up to do. Singapore, Indonesia, Japan, and Australia are well along in its deployment. France implemented ISDN in Brittany in 1987.

ISDN is primarily a concern of telecommunications providers, such as the Regional Bell Operating Companies in the United States and the national Poste Télégraphique and Téléphonique (PTTs) abroad. These provide the public network that is the infrastructure for consumer use and much of business use.

It is difficult to assess the business importance of ISDN or its likely future development and impact. One business alternative to ISDN is the corporate private network, which uses standards entirely different from ISDN. There have been delays in the filing and approving tariffs for ISDN in the United States, and ISDN investments and prices have

Many commentators define ISDN as "Items Subscribers Don't Need" or "Integrated Services Dream Network." Others define it as the next step beyond POTS—"Plain Old Telephone System."

created many regulatory arguments. Many regulators see ISDN as benefiting a few large businesses at the expense of the consumer base that will fund it.

See also: International Telecommunications, Network, Poste Télégraphique and Téléphonique, Telecommunications

Integration   Definitions and interpretations of integration vary; in general, integration refers to making the separate components of a technology base or business service work together and share resources. Today integration is a major priority in the IT industry, and there are many different approaches to providing it, ranging from standards for open systems to devices such as bridges, gateways, and protocol converters.

Although it is generally discussed in technical terms, integration is more important as a business concept. Most information technology applications in organizations have been built up over decades, using separate software, hardware, and telecommunications systems. These systems generally correspond to functional divisions in a company. Traditionally, finance, marketing, engineering, human resources, and so forth have had little need to cross-link their information and communication systems. But with the tidy separation of business functions beginning to break down, work and communication are becoming more interdependent across business operations. It is this business and organizational interdependence that is driving the need to integrate IT applications.

The degree of integration a firm achieves strongly influences its future business options. One major manufacturer's summary analysis of its IT capabilities is telling: it was spending $46 million per year on IT for its production department, which had many different systems, much homegrown software, and very high maintenance costs, yet the department was perceived to be increasingly unresponsive to customer requests. When it was discovered that the reason for this was that processing each order involved crossing multiple business functions, pulling the processes together became a business need, indeed an urgent business priority, for the firm. The process of doing so, which has involved throwing out some systems and equipment and redesign-

Integration is the opposite of incompatibility and the long-term goal for the IT field.

ing others, converting some systems to different software, and insisting that new development conform to specified technical standards, has so far taken eight years. It is not completed yet.

For any firm that does not already have an architecture in place, integration can be viewed as a three-stage process: (1) definition of a target architecture based on key, proven, and practical standards; (2) rationalization of existing systems; and (3) selective adoption of open standards as they are proven, while providing for continued operation of existing systems .

Technology integration is vital to the integration and cross-linking of business services and processes. It is the major opportunity and challenge for information technology in the 1990s.

See also: Architecture, Bridges, Routers, and Gateways, Compatibility, Connectivity, Open Systems, Platform, Standards, Systems Integration

Interface An interface is a connection between two devices. A wall outlet is the interface between electrical appliances and a power company's electric utility. IT standards relate largely to defining interfaces. For example, given a precise statement of the procedures and electrical signals for establishing a connection between a workstation and a local area network, hardware manufacturers, software developers, and local area network providers can design and implement their systems in many different ways with different internal features and, provided all conform to the interface standard, they will work together.

The key to defining and implementing standards is interfaces, not the specifics of products.

An effective architecture is built on standards that provide maximum clarity about interfaces and maximum freedom of choice in equipment and services.

See also: Bridges, Routers, and Gateways, Cables, Plugs, and Sockets, Integration, Open Systems, Protocol, Standards, Systems Integration, User Interface

International Telecommunications Internationally, telecommunications is usually handled by a highly regulatory, quasi-governmental agency termed a PTT, from the French Poste Télégraphique et Téléphonique. Most PTTs — some reluctantly, others willingly — are relaxing regulation ("liberalizing") in response to global trends in technology and business, among them British Telecom (a private company in a marketplace that is being opened to greater competition), France Telecom (very much a monopoly and an opponent of deregulation), Deutsche Bundespost (a recently reformed monopoly), and Japan's domestic NTT and KDD.

Widely varying prices resulting from the wide range of policies concerning liberalization have had major impacts on international firms' choices of location for back-office services. In international banking and securities, for example, London has gained at Germany's expense. London now processes 40 percent of the world's foreign exchange transactions, equal to Tokyo and New York combined. It holds this position primarily because of the quality, availability, and cost of its telecommunications services.

Europe's leading economy, Germany, is a laggard in telecommunications. Until recently it restricted business access to private networks and kept its telecommunications prices far higher than justified by its falling costs. To date, only about 15 percent of its telephone subscribers are linked to digital exchanges, compared to more than 90 percent in France. Catching up, and moving East Germany's primitive telecommunications infrastructure out of the 1950s, has become a German priority.

That competition in telecommunications immediately brings lower prices has been true in the deregulated U.S. long-distance market and in Japan, where the newest of three providers set its prices 23 percent lower than KDD's (Japan's former PTT), which responded within months with a 16 percent cut in rates. British Telecom has lowered its prices by 17 percent in real terms over a three-year period in response to competition from Mercury.

Telecommunications has become a contentious political issue and an increasingly important element in economic policy. It is analogous to the automobile industry in terms of capital costs, import/export and quota issues, and labor union concerns. PTTs' procurements tend to favor major national manufacturers, and trade wars in the $100-billion telecommunications equipment market are forcing many mergers and acquisitions.

International telecommunications expenditures grew by 600 percent in the 1980s and are on track to grow 500 percent in the 1990s. The **Financial Times** *reports that a country's telecommunications quality, cost, and availability are becoming a main indicator of its economic strength and growth.*

A major concern for transnational businesses is the lack of one-stop shopping for telecommunications. A company wanting to link French, Italian, Swedish, and U.S. operations must negotiate each end of each link with the appropriate PTT.

Business managers and information technology specialists cannot presume that international and domestic telecommunications will be similar in terms of cost, availability, quality, security, or technology. In some areas Europe is well ahead of the United States (e.g., Scandinavia in cellular communications, France in ISDN). In other areas it lags not so much in terms of technology, but in the responsiveness of the PTTs to business needs. Because the continent is starting from a smaller base of installed telephones, telecommunications growth has been and will continue to be far more rapid in Asia than in either Europe or North America. The geography of such countries as India and Indonesia calls for a mix of telecommunications strategies, with satellites playing a major role.

See also: Backbone Network, Cellular Communication, Mobile Communication, Network, Packet-Switching, Satellite, Telecommunications

ISDN   See Integrated Services Digital Network

IT   See Information Technology

Jargon and Acronyms   IT, like any other field, has its own language to differentiate options and features relevant to specific decisions. One well-respected desk reference book of computer terms contains more than 3,500 definitions, and it is by no means complete enough to cover the range of terms relevant to a typical large organization's IT resource.

The field is now so broad that technical specialists in one area are unlikely to be familiar with terms used by those in another.

The key to dealing with IT jargon is to know what you need to know. Specialists clearly need to know the jargon of their specialty and probably need to know a subset of the jargons of related specialties. This book presents a subset of IT terminology across all specialties that

Megaflops, phase jitter, fourth-order normal form, POSIX, GOSIP, ROM BIOS, OOPS, WYSIWYG, gender changer, fault tolerant, dithering, dialogue box, demand paging...some of the arcane vocabulary of IT has an almost poetic ring.

has relevance for business managers who need to be conversant in the discipline.

The danger with IT jargon is less with the esoteric terms than with the familiar terms that have different meanings in the IT field than in everyday life. "Architecture," "standard," and "system," for example, mean different things in different contexts. Relating them to issues of business integration and technical architecture provides the basis for a common context. A business manager should ask three simple questions about any term in the IT jargon: (1) Does it have any significance for our architecture or our ability to integrate business processes? (2) Which business opportunity or business impact does it represent? and (3) Does it require me, as a business manager, to rethink any aspect of my business plans?

Keyboard   See User Interface

Knowledge Engineering   See Expert System

Knowledge Representation   See Expert System

LAN   See Local Area Network

Laptop Computer   See Portable Computer

Local Area Network (LAN)   Local area networks or LANs, provide a means to link computers and workstations within a single location such as an office or building. LANs can be interconnected, with one another or with wide area networks (WANs), using interface devices called bridges, routers, and gateways.

Local area networks evolved as a subfield of telecommunications at a time when "telecom" meant primarily telephones. They were a response to the need for departmental personal computers to be able to share programs and data, data bases, and high-speed printers. This local need gradually expanded into an interdepartmental need, necessitating the development of devices for linking local area networks together and connecting them to wide area networks that could provide links to geographically dispersed LANs.

Initially, choices of local area networks were driven primarily by departmental needs, price, and ease of installation and operation. Demands for business and technical integration have made this case-by-case approach less practical. Increasingly departmental business needs and corporate needs must be handled together. Resolving the many incompatibilities among existing LANs and establishing LAN-WAN interconnections are among the most pressing problems in the IT field.

Smaller firms generally have different requirements for local area networks and fewer constraints than larger firms, which almost invariably have mainframe-based transaction processing systems and data resources and wide area networks linking geographically distributed locations. Well-established products such as Novell's Netware and Microsoft's LAN Manager are often sufficient to tie together the computing resources of a smaller firm using local communications. Ethernet and IBM's Token Ring network are more likely choices for firms that must integrate LANs into a wider computing and communications resource.

There is no "best" local area network; the choice depends on today's applications and tomorrow's need for extension and integration of applications across a firm's IT platform. Ethernet was by far the local area network most widely used by large firms in the 1980s. As of late 1990, the ratio between installations using Ethernet and those using IBM's Token Ring network was about 3:1.

Ethernet can move information at speeds of up to ten megabits (million) per second, although its practical rate of throughput is about two megabits per second, fast enough for simple applications that do not involve transfers of large volumes of data. Consequently, the simple-to-install Ethernet has remained a popular choice for departmental systems, particularly electronic mail and data base access even though IBM's Token Ring network offers higher speeds, typically from four to sixteen megabits per second. (The 1990 announcement of a new Ethernet standard called 10Base-T promises to extend its effective life.) Organizations that need higher speeds to handle complex, transaction-based applications are more likely to opt for the more expensive and complex to install and operate Token Ring network.

The current annual growth rate in units of local area networks is about 24 percent, with the growth in dollar sales under 10 percent.

The emerging generation of business applications, particularly those that use image processing and video, demands far greater capacity and faster transmission speeds than either Ethernet or Token Ring can support. FDDI, an emerging standard for fiber optics-based LANs, provides speeds of 100 megabits per second, which many commentators see as transitional.

Distinctions between local area networks, campus networks, metropolitan networks, and wide area networks are blurring. With specialized bridges, routers, and gateways, complicated wiring, interface boards that connect personal computers to LANs, and front-end processors and data switches that link LANs to wide area networks and remote services, what began as a simple concept of tying together systems within a building quickly, efficiently, and cheaply has turned into a morass of technical complexity. It is a critical issue that must be addressed in the corporate architecture at the level of corporate policy.

Many experts believe that local area networks represent the mainstream of telecommunications and that organizationwide networks will be built of interconnected LANs, using bridges and routers. That opinion should be respected; the growth in LAN capabilities over the past five years has been extraordinary. LANs can be used as the base for a telecommunications infrastructure that builds on the workstation as the core element of distributed computing and service. An alternative view, reflected in this guide, sees the backbone wide area network as the central component of the infrastructure, to which local area networks must be connected coherently and efficiently. Whichever view is adopted, integration of separate technology bases is the central goal.

See also: Architecture, Ethernet, FDDI, Integration, Network, Platform, Standards, Telecommunications, Token Ring, Transmission

Mainframe and Minicomputer

Because size and processing power have historically been correlated, the largest computers have been termed mainframes, those of intermediate size have been called minicomputers, and the smallest ones have been tagged microcomputers. An additional category, supercomputers, is begining to have relevance outside the research community in businesses such as telecommunications, which require extremely high-speed processing to manage the switching of extensive networks. Mainframe computers, usually centralized in data centers, have long been the workhorses of business computing. Today they are often connected to thousands of workstations that share the mainframe's resources through wide area telecommunications networks. Minicomputers targeted at departmental computing needs were a distinct market segment in the 1970s and 1980s.

Today, mainframes and minicomputers are more usefully viewed in the context of "distributed" systems, in which they function as "hosts" or "servers" to numerous and potentially widely scattered "client" workstations. In fact, with role becoming more relevant than size, client and server are a more useful distinction.

Each major computer vendor has been strongest in one segment of the mainframe/mini/micro market. IBM, for example, has long been seen as the provider of mainframes and protector of their role and market. Yet, sales of its mid-sized AS/400 machine amount to more than the entire company sales and profits of Digital Equipment Corporation (DEC), the number-two firm in the industry, and just as universally identified with minicomputers. Companies like Apple, Compaq, and Toshiba are firmly identified as providers of micro, or personal, computers.

Today, all vendors, regardless of their strength or market niche, must consider how well their products link to other elements of a firm's IT resources. Amdahl, Hitachi, and Fujitsu have sold their mainframe products on the basis of being IBM "plug compatible" — unplug an IBM machine and plug in one of theirs; the hardware fully supports the IBM operating system. Compaq has an edge over Apple with many companies because its personal computers can link directly into an IBM environment, and Apple and DEC are trying to create an edge by working together to make their products interlink.

As integrated and open — that is, vendor-independent — systems become a priority for leading customers, they also become a priority for vendors. In fact, some vendors, wanting to establish themselves as the preferred option within an integrated IT base, are competing on the basis of how vendor-independent their products are. Because of IBM's dominance of both the mainframe and personal computer markets,

Computers used to be classified by size—from mainframe to mini to micro. Many micros now have more raw computing power than mainframes, and distinctions among computers have come to relate more to their type of function than their size. The mainframe, for instance, is increasingly more the manager of large and complex data bases than the "computer."

many key business-processing systems now in use will be run on IBM equipment. Thus most vendors can be expected to make IBM-compatibility, IBM-connectability, or even IBM-substitutability a key element of their strategies.

See also: Architecture, Client/Server Model, Connectivity, Data Center, Distributed Systems, Host Computer, Network, Open Systems, Personal Computer, Platform, Supercomputer, Terminal, Workstation

Maintenance   Maintenance consumes 50–70 percent of staff resources of most Information Systems units. The term is in many ways a misnomer, suggesting routine repair and adjustment. Software maintenance is much more. It is a follow-on investment to development and installation that keeps a system functioning in its technical environment and current with the business requirements it was designed to address. A firm does not, for example, have the option of ignoring tax-law changes, but must make the necessary modifications to its payroll, pension, sales, and financial reporting systems. When the transactions processed by an existing application increase to a volume level that degrades performance, the system may have to be moved onto a larger computer or new telecommunications facilities added. Frequently, this requires changes to the computer programs.

All such accomplishments and revisions come under the heading of maintenance. Maintenance costs for a system will amount to from one to three times the original development cost. An old system that was insufficiently documented, has been modified many times, and was poorly designed to begin with is a programmer's nightmare to maintain. Unfortunately, many major transactions-processing systems possess all three of these characteristics.

For new development, the best solution to the maintenance problem is to improve design techniques and use tools that make programs self-documenting. For older systems, the problem is less tractable. Tools that restructure program code and generate accurate documentation have not as yet provided much payoff, though it is likely that they will do so eventually. In the meantime, existing systems must be maintained, diverting skilled staff away from development. Junior programmers learning their trade tend to view maintenance as a chore;

Only about 10 percent of an Information Services group's staff resources are available for developing new systems. Half or more are tied up in maintaining existing ones. Poor design, rushed testing, and inadequate documentation add up to an increased maintenance burden.

skilled application programmers who perceive themselves to be stuck in it, regard it as a major career blockage.

See also: Application Software and Application Development, Computer-Aided Software Engineering, Programming, Prototyping, Systems Life Cycle, Systems Programming, Testing

Management Information Systems (MIS)

Management information systems, or MIS, is a catch-all term used to describe mainstream computer use in the 1970s and 1980s. MIS replaced the "data processing" focus on automation of clerical activities with an emphasis on providing paper-based information for management reporting, planning, and control. Today, the term "Information Systems" is more frequently used, partly because the MIS era provided managers a great deal of paper but very little information.

The principal sources of information through the mid-1980s were companies' internal transaction-processing systems. Most were batch systems, run daily, weekly, or monthly, depending on the application. The information these systems provided management was only as timely as the frequency of processing. It was also based largely on historical accounting data.

As on-line systems, data-base management systems, personal computers, and easy-to-use software became available, new approaches to providing managers with meaningful and timely information emerged, approaches that were deliberately contrasted with MIS. The earliest of these were decision support systems, small-scale systems based on analytic modeling techniques such as simulation, forecasting, and financial projection, that were designed to meet individual managers' needs. Executive information systems added a new focus on capturing and manipulating the data most relevant to top managers' needs — for example, external competitive data and key operational indicators.

The most recent and far-reaching extension of decision support and executive information systems is the use of point-of-event data capture to move information to a central data store where it can be accessed from personal computers. Point of event includes point of sale in retailing, point of reservation in airlines and hotels, and point of order in manufacturing. As firms' core systems process transactions,

Traditional management information systems had little to do with management, were accumulations of accounting data, and seldom added up to a comprehensive system of tools. Today's systems focus on alerting managers to problems and trends, answering their ad hoc questions, and providing information in the form they want, when they want it.

they send the data to the central system, often immediately, but certainly no later than end of day, providing management information that is completely up-to-date.

Leading retailers such as The Limited and Toys "R" Us use this approach to manage their entire logistical system on a continuous basis, enabling them to spot trends within days, know the details of every product in every store, and link their systems with those of suppliers, shortening the replenishment cycle. Systems that provide such capability are management alerting rather than management reporting systems. Top management of retailers that have come to dominate a market niche, without exception, view the information provided by such systems as a priority.

See also: Computer-Integrated Manufacturing, Computerized Reservation System, Decision Support System, Executive Information System, On-Line Transaction Processing, Point of Sale

Macintosh   See Personal Computer

Megahertz and Gigahertz   Megahertz and gigahertz are high-bandwidth radio frequencies that define the information-carrying capacity of telecommunications facilities such as satellites and the speed of the internal circuits of central processing units.

See also: Bandwidth, Central Processing Unit, Fiber Optics, Satellite, Transmission

Microcomputer   See Personal Computer

Millions of Instructions per Second (MIPS)   Millions of instructions per second, or MIPS, is a rough measure of the power of a computer, rather like horsepower is an approximate measure of the performance of an automobile engine. In 1980, IBM's top-of-the-line computers provided 4.5 MIPS for $4.5 million. By 1990, the cost of a MIP on a personal computer had dropped to $1,000, driving the trend toward "distributing" computing power, instead of relying solely on large central machines. But MIPS, like horsepower, are an incomplete indicator of capability. The answer to the frequently asked question "If

Amdahl, Hitachi, and IBM announced increases in the processing capacity of their top-of-the-line mainframe computers from 200 MIPS in 1991 to well over 300 MIPS in 1992. In mid-1990, power workstations were in the 10–30 MIP range, in mid-1991, Hewlett-Packard took the lead with a 75-MIP workstation. While MIPS is increasingly no more precise a descriptor of a computer's quality and performance than is horsepower a descriptor of a car's, the figure is useful as a measure of year-to-year progress and cost improvement.

we can put 50 MIPS on the desk, who needs mainframes?" is "Lots of people." Mainframes remain essential for many aspects of information management and coordination.

The limitation of MIPS as the single measure of capability of a computer is illustrated by comparing two widely used machines. The $350,000 Digital Equipment Corporation VAX 8530 minicomputer is rated at 4 MIPS and the $35,000 Compaq SystemPro personal computer at 12 MIPS. Is the Compaq system a better buy? A systems manager contemplating a purchase had better not answer before learning that the VAX can handle input and output ("I/O") from disk storage to computer memory far faster than the SystemPro and, depending on the mix of I/O and number-crunching, may be many times faster. MIPS is most appropriately used to compare computers within a given type, such as large mainframes or personal computers.

See also: Central Processing Unit, Mainframe and Minicomputer, Personal Computer, Portable Computer, Supercomputer

Millisecond and Microsecond   The speed at which components of computing and communications facilities operate varies widely. Watches record seconds because that is the smallest unit of time in which humans operate. Disks operate at speeds measured in milliseconds (thousandths of a second), computers process at speeds measured in microseconds (millionths of a second), and chips function at speeds measured in nanoseconds (billionths of a second) and picoseconds (trillionths of a second).

Much of the complexity of the design and operation of an IT resource relates to coordinating and synchronizing components that run at entirely different speeds in order to ensure that none becomes a bottleneck to others. If we artificially redefined a nanosecond to be an hour, a millisecond becomes 41 days and a second 112 years; it becomes easy to see how a nanosecond speed CPU might be kept sitting idle while a disk accesses data at millisecond speeds.

See also: Central Processing Unit, Chip, Satellites, Telecommunications, Transmission

Computers compute in microseconds, but move information in and out to disk in milliseconds. That means that a faster computer may not mean faster processing, if the machine is "I/O bound"— this is rather like a traffic jam at the toll booth.

MIPS   See Millions of Instructions per Second

MIS　See Management Information Systems

Mobile Communication　Wireless telecommunications transmission is termed mobile communication because it can accommodate continuous changes in the physical locations of sender and receiver. This is the mechanism by which cars, ships, and aircraft receive communications while in motion. The most common transmission medium for mobile communication is radio frequency signals broadcast via terrestrial microwave (particularly for cellular telephones) or satellite facilities.

The emerging extension of mobile (hence cableless and location-independent) communications is wireless local area networks. Cabling buildings is expensive, complicated, and often slow. Some older buildings are unsuited to it. The senior manager looking admiringly at an architect's design for a new office complex is well advised to keep in mind that a building now must be configured on the assumption that there will be at least one workstation for every two staff who work in it. Wireless LANs using radio frequency signals or infrared beams can facilitate the movement of personal computers around an office building and reduce the need for cabling.

Mobile communication is one of the obvious major waves of innovation emerging in the 1990s. Among the problems making it slow in forming are regulation, standards, supplier stability, and FCC allocation of radio frequencies for transmission.

See also: *Cellular Communication, International Telecommunications, Local Area Network, Satellite, Standard, Switch, Telecommunications*

There can be no doubt that wireless communications will be an explosive growth area sometime in the 1990s. The technology is moving fast, federal government regulators are considering auctioning off rights to use the radio frequency spectrum, and the computer technology for personal communications networks (PCNs) is available. This is a little like Hollywood in the 1920s; someone will get very rich, but who?

Modem　A modem is a device that makes it possible to link a digital computer to the analog telephone system. It "modulates" a computer's digital bit stream into an analog signal that can be transmitted over telephone lines and "demodulates" incoming analog signals into digital bit streams; hence "modem" for modulator/demodulator.

A modem determines the speed at which information can be transmitted and received. A standard "voice-grade" telephone line is capable of carrying data at speeds of up to 9,600 bits per second, but most personal computer modems operate at only 1,200 or 2,400 bits per second. Data centers often employ high-speed modems that operate at 19,200 or even 38,400 bits per second and may provide additional features such as data compression, automatic redialing, and error control.

Modems also perform a variety of technical functions. For example, they match the characteristics of the sending device's transmission with those of the receiving device. Hayes and Hayes-compatible modems, which relieve users of most of the work involved in defining transmission speeds and protocols, dominate the personal computer market.

Modems are essential today for enabling firms to make efficient use of transmission links. Eventually, as digital networks come to predominate, they will go the way of the punched card.

See also: Digital, Network, Telecommunications

Monitor See User Interface

Mouse See User Interface

MS.DOS MS.DOS is the operating system that was responsible for transforming the personal computer into a standard tool for business and professional activities and creating the base for today's massive personal computer software industry. Once IBM adopted MS.DOS as the operating system for its own product, software designers practically ceased to develop software for rival operating systems, which helped to establish MS.DOS as the dominant operating system in business use.

The limitations of MS.DOS lie in its original design, which limited the size of programs that could run under it to 640K of memory, a huge amount at the time but trivial today. It is also, in comparison with the operating systems of later personal computers such as the Apple Macintosh, difficult to learn and cumbersome to use.

MS.DOS is the last and greatest product of the 1970s' approach to developing software. It makes the user rather than the operating system handle complexity; it is intolerant of mistakes and obscure in its responses; it is devoid of grace or charm. In short, it represents just about everything people have come to dislike about computers.

The world's telephone systems were designed around a technology that transmitted information in a form entirely different from how computer information was coded. Modems are the necessary device for making the conversion. The new "digital" networks do not need them.

Nevertheless, it remains the work horse of professional users and is compatible with a wealth of available software.

Many personal computer users who find MS.DOS good enough have not converted to the newer generation of IBM PCs, which run a different operating system, called OS/2. Many newer software packages for MS.DOS machines simplify its use through graphical user interfaces that make interaction more like that with a Macintosh. The many portable lap top computers that have flooded the market in the past few years mostly run MS.DOS, thus further extending its likely lifetime.

See also: Operating System, Personal Computer, Portable Computer

Nanosecond   See Millisecond and Microsecond

Network   Networks are the telecommunications highways over which information travels. The information can originate from and be directed to all manner of devices, including telephones, televisions, satellites, sensors and alarms, and computers of all sizes and descriptions, ranging from large mainframes to minicomputers to personal computers and specialized workstations such as automated teller machines and automated cash registers. In effect, a network is a directory of contact points that operates much like the public telephone network, which publishes its contact points as telephone numbers in a directory. Although networks can be connected internationally in the same way that international telephone systems can be connected, the problems associated with linking networks built on entirely different transmission techniques and technology bases are daunting.

Networks are variously described in terms of their geographic extent and ownership. A local area network, or LAN, connects devices in close physical proximity — for example, within an office or building. Transmission media for LANs include wire, coaxial, and fiber optic cable. Devices connected to a LAN, termed "nodes," require a special interface card. LANs are connected to one another via "bridges," "routers," and "gateways." Bridges and routers connect like networks (i.e., networks that use the same transmission protocol), the latter having the added ability to select the least-congested and least-expensive route. Gateways are more complex devices used to connect dissimilar networks. All of these devices add overhead, which is likely to degrade performance as well as add cost.

The technology of local area networks limits the geographic distance they can cover. Metropolitan, intercity, national, or international networks need long-distance transmission facilities such as are provided by telephone companies or satellite transmission. Networks that span such distances are termed wide area networks. To overcome the weakening, or attenuation, of signals transmitted beyond a certain distance, "repeaters" are employed.

Wide area networks can be either private or public. Private networks are fixed-cost services leased from a telecommunications provider such as AT&T, MCI, or US Sprint in the United States, British Telecom or Mercury in Britain, and various national communications providers elsewhere that guarantee levels of capacity and performance. With a private network and skilled network managers, a company can manage its communications traffic so as to achieve the maximum rate of throughput at a fixed cost. A variant of the private network is called the "virtual private" or "software defined" network.

Public data networks, or PDNs, provide small and large firms alike with easy access to telecommunications transmission services. Users pay as they go; the more traffic they put through the network, the more they pay. Regional and national telephone services are examples of public data networks. Outside of the United States, public data networks continue to predominate because of the far slower pace of deregulation, which creates alternatives to public networks.

A commercial network that adds something of value to transmission — electronic data interchange services, electronic mail, information services, and so forth — is termed a value-added network, or VAN. VANs are more common in Europe than in the United States, largely because industries there have worked more closely together to share resources, whereas larger U.S. firms have tended to build their own "private" facilities. The growing importance of intra-industry and intercompany electronic transactions is making VANs an attractive option, especially in the international area, where they are referred to

If 25–80 percent of a firm's cash flow is on-line, as it is for all banks and airlines, most manufacturers and retailers, and many insurance firms, the company's business strategy suddenly becomes totally irrelevant when the network is down.

as IVANs. VANs are particularly useful for intra-industry transactions such as electronic data interchange and payments systems.

Although it is the key enabler of business innovation and the strategic infrastructure for business in the 1990s, telecommunications is still too often thought of as part of operational overhead. For airlines and banks, the network is the franchise for their products and customer service. For manufacturers, it is the coordinator of just-in-time operations. For distribution-intensive companies, it is the basis for customer service.

Although stand-alone computers and local area networks can provide benefits to individual users and departments, the creation of a business resource that links them, shares their business capabilities, and facilitates cross-functional, cross-locational, and cross-product services and operations relies on the development of a more pervasive network architecture.

A key part of this architecture is the backbone network. This is an organization's central information highway system, which can be shared by many business units and many applications. It can be likened to the principal routes of a major airline, which connect with smaller, subsidiary feeder lines (analogous to local area networks) and the routes of other major airlines (analogous to supplier, customer, and public data networks).

See also: Architecture, Backbone Network, Bandwidth, Ethernet, International Telecommunications, Local Area Network, Mobile Communication, Platform, Packet-Switching, Poste Télégraphique and Téléphonique, Protocol, Public Data Network, Telecommunications, Token Ring, Transmission, Value-Added Network, Wide Area Network

"If the human aspect of networking doesn't get you, the networking side will." —Debra Townes, "When Bad Things Happen to Good Files," Network Computing, March 1991

Network Management   Network management is one of the most vital aspects of managing an on-line business service. Complex electronic processing bases that support many subscribers are often built on an extensive array of equipment and transmission facilities. The monitoring of diagnostics, management alerting and reporting, and even repair of such facilities is increasingly being handled by automated network management systems.

The average business experiences two hours of network downtime per week, according to a 1990 *Benchmarks* magazine survey. This is equivalent to 12 days per year. Ten percent of large and 6 percent of smaller businesses in the study put the cost of this downtime at between $5,000 and $50,000 per hour, between $500,000 and $5 million per year. These are significant losses.

Because network failures now constitute business failures, network management is a strategic business issue and skills in network management and automated network systems are crucial investments. Automated network management tools have become vital to large organizations that manage computerized reservation, computer-integrated manufacturing, or retailing point-of-sale systems that rely on a variety of devices, transmission links, and switching equipment functioning at levels above 99.9 percent availability and reliability. There are as yet no established standards for network management and the existing tools are fragmented and limited.

See also: Architecture, Distributed Systems, Maintenance, Network, Platform, Security, Switch, Telecommunications, Transmission

Notebook Computer   See Personal Computer

Object-Oriented Programming Systems (OOPS)   Object-oriented programming systems, or OOPS, address one of the longest standing concerns in IT — how to improve the quality of software and the productivity of software development. It takes a building-block approach to program development. Each block, termed an object, is independent and able to run by itself or be simply and automatically interlocked with other objects. Entire systems can be created that reuse existing objects, and, because they are independent, each object can be changed without affecting others. The concept, though simple, transforms both the methods of systems development and the tools for programming.

Objects interact by passing information between one another. For example, an object that calculates the rate of return on an investment might link to an object that displays a graph of the results. The first object needs know nothing about how the second plots the graph. Each object must contain information about itself ("encapsulation") and the

This may—just may— be the long-awaited breakthrough in systems design and development. It uses a Lego-block approach to linking "objects" together. The objects may be data bases, software routines, videos, photos, music, or communications commands.

objects it can relate to ("inheritance"). The vocabulary of object-oriented programming includes classes and subclasses, parents and subordinate objects. Its specialized programming languages include Smalltalk, C, and C++.

See also: *Application Software and Application Development, Computer-Aided Software Engineering, Programming, Prototyping, Software, Systems Programming, Testing*

OLTP   See On-Line Transaction Processing

On-Line   On-line is a term used to indicate that data is immediately and directly accessible from a computer or workstation. It contrasts with off-line, which indicates that data is stored on an external device such as a magnetic tape or floppy disk and must be loaded into a computer for the program or service that needs it.

See also: *Batch Processing, On-Line Transaction Processing*

On-Line Transaction Processing   On-line transaction processing has supplanted batch processing in most time-sensitive applications. In banking, for example, customer account information has to be put on-line in order for deposits and withdrawals made at automated teller machines to be transacted immediately. Because it incurs added costs for overhead and for ensuring security, back up, adequate response time, and the ability to manage highly variable processing loads, on-line transaction processing tends to be much more expensive than batch processing. One major bank has calculated that the 4,000 lines of software code per customer required by the batch systems that handled current account processing grew to 44,000 lines per customer in the on-line environment of automated teller machines and to 120,000 lines per customer to handle processing from other banks' ATMs.

Although batch processing remains a viable alternative for applications such as payroll, every system that is part of just-in-time business and customer service is likely to move on-line. Indeed, on-line transaction processing was a prerequisite for such innovative services as automated airline reservation and point-of-sale systems.

See also: *Electronic Funds Transfer at Point of Sale, On-Line, Point of Sale, Terminal*

American Airlines and United Airlines process close to two thousand transactions a second through their reservation systems. Their network is their business franchise. An airline without access to on-line reservation processing is like a bank without checkbooks—or a bank without on-line automated teller machines for transaction processing.

OOPS   See Object-Oriented Programming Systems

Open Systems   Users and vendors have a mutual need for vendor- and product-independent standards. "Open systems" are implicitly vendor-independent and, by extension, interconnectable and "interoperable." The problem is how to get to open systems from the preponderance of proprietary systems.

The primary blueprint for a general framework for open systems is Open Systems Interconnection, or OSI. The object of OSI is to make all devices and services interoperable. Progress toward OSI has been steady but slow and there remain many problems of definition as well as implementation. Limited other frameworks for open systems are being developed in specific areas of IT.

A practical definition of an open system standard includes four parts. It must (1) be fully defined, allowing vendors and suppliers of services to work from the same definition, (2) be stable, affording vendors and suppliers a fixed instead of rapidly moving target, (3) fully publish its interfaces so that they are accesssible to vendors and suppliers, and (4) not be subject to control by any one player. This is not the definition used by many telecommunications specialists, who tend, instead, to view open systems in terms of the formal proposals by standard-setting committees that lead to agreements on definitions of a standard. They ignore the issues of implementing the defined standard which frequently results in so many variations in features, products, or interpretation of the standard that the variants are in effect proprietary. In practice, open systems are often created through overwhelming customer demand for a particular product, which leads other vendors to tailor their products to it. Thus what is established as a "proprietary" standard can become an open standard in terms of implementation. MS.DOS is an example of this.

However defined, open systems are the key to the future of information technology. They will most likely come about through a combination of committee definitions, de facto standards created by user demand, and vendor decisions about which committee and competitor standards to follow.

See also: *Architecture, Compatibility, Integration, Interface, Open Systems Interconnection, Standards, Systems Integration*

Photocopiers are partly built on open standards; when you buy photocopying paper, you do not need to specify the specific make and brand of machine; they all use 8 ½" by 11" paper. You will have to specify the machine when you buy a toner cartridge; that is proprietary.

Open Systems Interconnection (OSI)   Open systems Interconnection, or OSI, is the major framework for creating vendor- and equipment-independent systems that can work together. Conceived in Europe in the 1970s, OSI was adopted in the mid-1980s by telecommunications and computer vendors as a consensual direction toward resolving the long unsolvable problems of incompatibility. The plan is for OSI to create a reference model that can be used by designers of telecommunications networks and networking equipment to develop equipment and services that might be entirely different in terms of technology but will be able to work together.

OSI is only a blueprint. It does not specify how systems should interconnect, only the interfaces for doing so, which it defines as a series of seven layers. Layer 1 specifies the interface for establishing a physical connection between a sender and receiver, layer 2 the interface for transmitting data between them.

The concept of layers is central to both OSI and IBM's competing systems network architecture (SNA). Each layer is complete in itself, with control passed from a layer to the one above. Designers of equipment that interfaces at level 1 need know nothing about how equipment that interfaces at level 2 operates. The lowest layers are proving the easiest to implement because they address physical interconnections and build on well-established standards. The higher levels define interfaces for transaction formats and procedures for handling application requests. Progress here is slow and fragmented. The layered architecture has enabled OSI subcommittees to work independently on individual standards within the reference model.

Once defined, an OSI standard must be implemented in real products. Because the details of the standard must cover so many contingencies and types of activity, there will invariably be differences in how that is done. In late 1990, a group of aerospace industry users discovered that vendors' implementations of FTAM, one OSI standard, were incompatible, preventing them from exchanging certain types of files. *Communications Week* for November 1990 observed that "The problems with FTAM are...a microcosm of the challenges ahead for businesses and organizations implementing OSI products. The myriad attractive features offered as options within each OSI standard also can backfire on users, leaving them with implementations that can't even communicate."

The business jury is still out on OSI. Telecommunications specialists and computer scientists tend to be more optimistic than most Information Systems managers. It is likely that OSI will never be implemented in its entirety, but will continue to provide a basis for building stable and reasonably open components of the IT resource. It has provided sufficient impetus for reducing incompatibility to lead IBM, regarded by many OSI proponents as the dragon of proprietariness, to make many of its new products "OSI-compliant."

There is no open systems tooth fairy. OSI will not suddenly be complete and instantly implemented. It will no doubt be a major element in the evolution of open systems, but it will be overtaken by new developments in IT. The original definition of OSI did not encompass network management, for example. New subcommittees rushed to include it, but network management products were developed ahead of the standards.

The best advice one can provide to nontechnical business managers about OSI is that it represents a long-term movement toward true open systems and that its overall goals are more important than its details. Full implementation will take a decade or more, if it is ever achieved. Managers should recognize that there are no shortcuts to open systems and integration. Ask IS managers not, "Why aren't we implementing OSI?" but rather, "How does our architecture balance the constraints of old investments, uncertainty about the direction and progress of standards, and the opportunities of OSI?" The architecture, not OSI, is the strategy, although OSI may be a key element of the architecture.

See also: Architecture, Open Systems, Platform, Standards

For many years, OSI has been as much a subject of quasi-religious frenzy as a technical issue. There are true believers, agnostics, zealots, and skeptics with an underlying pro- and anti-IBM political subtext. The hype has been at times absurd, and progress slow, but the OSI model has generated several of the most important and useful standards in the telecommunications field.

Operating System An operating system is an extensive and complex set of programs that manages the operation of a computer and the applications that run on it. Mainframe operating systems are among the most complex intellectual artefacts ever created, requiring literally thousands of man years to develop and thousands more to maintain and enhance.

A computer is defined more by its operating system than any other single feature. Effective progress in exploiting hardware and software is paced or blocked by existing, evolving, and emerging operating systems.

Major mainframe operating systems include MVS, DOS/VSE, OS/400, and VM for IBM computers and VMS for Digital Equipment Corporation computers. Among personal computers, IBM's MS.DOS has become a de facto standard. Its more recent OS/2 operating system is not yet compatible with MS.DOS, and Apple's Macintosh operating system is incompatible with both. UNIX, a specialized operating system developed by Bell Labs and licensed for general use, is growing in popularity, particularly among users of high-end workstations.

All mainframe and high-end minicomputer vendors share a common set of problems in developing new operating systems: how to ensure that user firms can continue to run existing applications while migrating older operating systems toward open standards. IBM's systems application architecture (SAA) is an ambitious attempt to provide a set of interfaces that pull together its main operating systems. Digital Equipment Corporation, Hewlett-Packard, UNISYS, NCR, and other leading vendors plan to offer equivalent facilities; it will be several years before they are in place.

Historically, computer operating systems have been entirely proprietary — confined to a specific vendor's products. Because many vendors have introduced multiple and incompatible operating systems, a new generation of hardware has often meant a new operating system and the adaptation or even rewriting of existing applications. Four major forces are working to change this. One, as standards for open systems are developed and reduce incompatibility among IT components, the choice of operating system will become less restricting. Two, a strong advocacy is emerging among technical specialists and many vendors for UNIX as the most "portable" operating system. Three, many vendors have made a strategic choice to make their own products compatible with those of IBM, which have by virtue of their dominance of the mainframe and personal computer markets become de facto standards. Four, IBM has accepted that its proprietary systems must incorporate the principal open standards and be able to link to other vendors' products.

See also: *Central Processing Unit, Compatibility, Mainframe and Minicomputer, MS.DOS, OS/2, Personal Computer, Portable Computer, Proprietary, Standards*

Optical Disk   See Compact Disc-Read Only Memory

Optical Fiber   See Fiber Optics

OSI   See Open Systems Interconnection

OS/2   IBM developed the OS/2 operating system for its PS/2 series of personal computers. OS/2 supports "multitasking," that is, running more than one application simultaneously and "multithreading," which means that it can initiate several processes at once within a single application.

There is a widely held view among many personal computer users and commentators that Microsoft Windows has severely damaged the prospects of OS/2. The opinion of a sizable plurality of top IS planners and executives, however, is that OS/2 is essential for the multimedia applications they are planning.

See also: MS.DOS, Operating System

Outsourcing   Outsourcing is the practice of contracting with an outside firm that can afford to hire top technical specialists by spreading their time over a number of contracts. The outside firm may run part or all of a company's IT operations, including networks, data centers, maintenance, and/or software development.

Outsourcing is variously viewed as a means of reducing costs, offloading work to enable a firm to concentrate on a smaller number of critical aspects of IT development and use, and accessing expensive skills that would be too expensive to provide in-house. Seeking a long-term commitment to fixed-price services can further reduce costs. Outsourcing firms eager to gain market share are often willing to cut prices for the first few years, betting on their ability to increase efficiency and reduce their own costs.

Many nonstrategic aspects of IT operations can be efficiently and effectively contracted out. The argument most often raised against outsourcing is that the firm risks losing control over a key business resource. But the complexity of outsourcing should also not be overlooked. Contracts that ensure that all relevant levels of service,

No commentator is quite sure which aspects of outsourcing are a fad, what the real risks and benefits are, or the appropriate criteria for selecting an outsourcer.

quality, and responsiveness are explicitly stated often run to thousands of pages. Outsourcing has become highly controversial in IS circles. Firms fearful of losing control of strategic elements of IT relevant to competitive positioning liken outsourcing of IT to outsourcing of R&D.

Outsourcing is a relatively new term, but in practice most large Information Systems organizations have been multisourced for many years. No firm can afford all the IT resources or locate all the essential expertise it needs. Many contract out some aspects of systems development, participate in shared industry networks, and have special arrangements with suppliers for service and maintenance. This being the case, outsourcing versus in-house management is less an either/or than a both/and issue.

The decision to outsource some or all of a firm's core IT development and operations is a major one and not easily reversed. Senior business executives in most firms are likely to see it on the agenda several times in the next few years.

See also: Application Software and Application Development, Data Center, Maintenance, Network Management

Package   A software package is a set of programs that can be bought off the shelf and used as is or modified to meet specific needs of the purchaser. Packages usually address a particular, usually generic, business application, vary widely in quality, and frequently require as much planning as customized software development.

Too many firms underestimate the extent to which they will have to adapt work processes to use a package effectively or modify a package to fit the work at hand. No package can economically provide sufficient flexibility to accommodate all the variants in firms' business processes. In evaluating the trade-offs between purchasing a package and developing a system in-house, a company must examine the interdependencies among the software and its own organization, work flows, skills, and informal communications, and the strengths and availability of its own systems development staff. Such an analysis will help a firm to make a purchase or begin development with a clear organizational as well as technical plan.

See also: Application Software and Application Development, Programming, Prototyping, Software

Packet-Switching   Widely used by public data-communications networks, packet-switching is a technique whereby large messages are split into small, fixed-length units, or packets, for transmission. Each packet contains the necessary information to route it through the network, handle any transmission errors, and ensure that it is reassembled with its constituent packets into the original message at its destination.

This "bursty" traffic can be efficiently and cheaply moved across the nodes of a large wide area network. The alternative, circuit-switching is more suited to transmitting large units of data that need synchronization of sending and receiving equipment.

The principal standard for packet-switching is X.25. It is nearly impossible for a firm to develop an international telecommunications infrastructure that does not include X.25, because there are so many countries in which the only access to wide area network transmission is through the public X.25 data network.

See also: International Telecommunications, Network, Protocol, Standards, Telecommunications, Transmission, Wide Area Network, X.25

PC   See Personal Computer

PDN   See Public Data Network

Personal Computer   Originally just that — a self-contained computer designed to be used by a single individual — personal computers today are viewed increasingly by business as part of a larger information infrastructure; hence the growing emphasis on networking, interactive program and data sharing, and distributed computing.

Personal computers are small and getting smaller. They range from television-sized desktop machines to laptop computers that weigh about 12 pounds and newer notebook computers that weigh as little as 2 pounds.

A personal computer comprises both hardware and software. Hardware includes the central processing unit and main memory in which programs are run, the screen or monitor on which information is displayed, and disk drives from which programs and data are transferred into the central processing unit and memory, as well as peripheral devices such as printers and scanners. Software includes operating systems (e.g., OS/2, MS.DOS, and UNIX), utility programs (e.g., for copying or sorting files or retrieving files from damaged disks), and application programs (e.g., spreadsheet, statistical analysis, and word processing programs).

Personal computers today generally follow three "streams"— IBM personal computers, IBM-compatible personal computers (marketed by firms such as Compaq, Zenith, and others), and Apple personal computers — plus one rivulet, UNIX-based computers. IBM leveraged its long-time dominance of the mainframe computer arena to carve out a sizable chunk of the business market for personal computers. Apple had a harder time building market share for its Macintosh computer, which featured a more intuitive, graphical, icon-oriented user interface. The Macintosh built a strong base of individual users of personal computers but its deliberate decision to make the Mac incompatible with any other system slowed its adoption by large organizations. Contenders for the compatibles market hitched their generally cheaper machines to IBM's star, making sure that any standard software that runs on a true blue IBM PC runs on theirs.

An IBM personal computer comparable in power to a $1,000 portable computer in the United States sells for 60,000 rubles in the USSR, twice President Gorbachev's annual salary. PCs are traded on the new Moscow Commodities Exchange alongside wheat and oil.

The advantages of the Mac's graphical user interface in terms of ease of use and speed of learning have made it a target for imitation. By choosing to shift the complexity of operations from the user to the machine, Apple changed the philosophy of computing, and IBM and IBM-compatible computers increasingly incorporated Apple-like user interfaces. A software package introduced by Microsoft in 1990 that turns an IBM or IBM-compatible personal computer into a Macintosh look-alike sold more than a million copies in six months.

The business manager must attend closely to the rapid evolution of personal computing. Prices fluctuate. New capabilities emerge; user and system interfaces are enhanced and extended. The manager must evaluate these considerations in light of organizational needs and the importance of consistency and integration with other elements of the firm's technical base.

See also: *MS.DOS, OS/2, Portable Computer, Terminal, UNIX, User Interface*

Platform   An IT platform is a shared delivery base for a wide range of IT-based services. It suggests an approach that begins with defining an architecture that interconnects applications and allows them to share data automatically and directly, as an alternative to the traditional approach of developing separate and almost invariably incompatible applications, The history of information technology use in large organizations in the 1980s was principally one of independent technology bases for specific business functions with local needs driving the choice of hardware, software, and telecommunications. Today, there is growing recognition that there needs to be a larger focus on linking local systems to ensure that cross-functional business operations are supported by cross-functional IT systems.

It is impossible to build a shared platform without a corporate architecture.

See also: *Architecture, Integration*

Plugs   See Cables, Plugs, and Sockets

Point of Sale (POS)   Point of sale, or POS, refers to the on-line linking of sales transactions with planning, ordering, pricing, inventory management, and other business functions. In a point-of-sale system, as a business transaction occurs, information flows to other relevant planning and operational areas of the business. Increasingly, POS systems are being linked to financial networks, primarily for credit card authorization.

Equipment at the point-of-sale end of POS systems usually includes computerized cash registers and such ancilliary devices as bar code scanners and credit card readers. These POS terminals are linked to a store or central computer, allowing sales, inventory, and pricing data to be updated immediately. This capability can be used to support just-in-time purchasing, alert management to shifts in consumer patterns, reduce errors, monitor sales promotions, rapidly update prices, and generally improve effectiveness and efficiency.

Like computerized reservation systems and automated teller machines, point-of-sale systems, demand high reliability, high-speed telecommunications facilities, and powerful data-base management

Toys "R" Us can spot a sales trend in days. The point-of-sale system lets managers know what customers are buying on a daily basis. In 1986, Toys "R" Us tried out yellow scooters with a small order of 10,000. They sold out in two days; the computers spotted this from the POS data and automatically reordered. The firm sold a million scooters.

and transaction processing systems. Tandem Computer has created an effective niche by providing "fault tolerant" systems built around sets of linked machines that work in parallel; if one goes down, another immediately picks up the work.

See also: *Distributed Systems, Electronic Data Interchange, Electronic Funds Transfer at Point of Sale, On-Line Transaction Processing*

Portable Computer   Portable computers are small but powerful computers that weigh between two and twenty pounds; most fit into a briefcase. They consitute one of the fastest-growing segments of the personal computer market.

The primary advantage of portable computers is obviously their portability; they can be used almost anywhere. Many operate on batteries that last from two to four hours between rechargings. Portable computers cost more than equivalent desktop machines, and most have smaller screens that are backlit to make the screen images crisp and easy to read. They are available in a variety of sizes, variously termed laptop, notebook, and hand-held computers.

The typical middleweight laptop runs the MS.DOS operating system and can run the leading desktop word processing, spreadsheet, and data-base management packages. It comes with a hard disk that stores from 20 to 40 megabytes of data, and includes a modem that enables it to be connected to the telephone system through a standard jack.

Lightweight printers weighing about two pounds can be connected to a laptop and will generally fit beside it in a briefcase. Portable scanners, fax, and other add-on devices are also available. Battery life and recharging rarely live up to the manufacturers' promises, and many rechargers seem to weigh ten times what the laptop weighs.

The laptop market is ferociously competitive in both quality and price. Good machines cost about $1,000, superb machines less than $5,000. Compaq, Toshiba, Zenith, Grid, and many lesser-known names offer comparable laptops and face a continuing problem of differentiation. Because laptops are assembled largely from purchased components from many sources (and countries) it is almost impossible for any manufacturer to establish a sustainable edge. In mid-1990, several suppliers introduced machines based on the Intel 386 chip that would have been top-of-the-line desktops just a year earlier. They were duplicated within months.

Laptops are a buyer's market. They are also a necessity for many executives, consultants, sales reps, writers, lawyers, and other professionals who no longer have to leave critical files and software in their offices when they travel.

With respect to price, simple mathematics show that it is worth investing 65 percent of an individual's salary in a personal computer, laptop or desktop, to gain an average of one hour per day of more effective work. That amounts to close to $20,000 for someone earning $35,000 per year. This guide was written entirely on a laptop and would have taken at least an extra six months to create without it.

Even smaller notebook computers weighing two pounds or less have swept the market in recent years. Their principal limitation is keyboard and screen size, which has led a few manufacturers to introduce models that include a light pen for writing directly on the the screen. Notebook computers, though slow and limited in capability, represent the logical next development in the innovative and highly competitive personal computer market. Notebook computers and lightpen input are a major area of development in Japan, where the nature of the language and its characters makes keyboard-based input largely impractical.

Hand-held computers, the smallest of the portable computers, are special-purpose machines widely used in retailing and distribution. They are robust, able to withstand shocks, dust, and beverage spillage. Supermarket clerks use hand-helds to check inventory and input orders; Federal Express delivery staff use them to record package pick ups. Most hand-helds incorporate a bar code reader and will generally upload data to central computers via a telecommunications link.

See also: Bar Code, Modem, MS.DOS, Personal Computer

Information technology is really about convenience. Automated teller machines and portable fax took off for this reason. A computer in your briefcase is convenient. Until 1990, laptops were heavy, their screens hard to read, and their performance very limited. They now combine convnience with power and ease of use.

POS   See Point of Sale

Poste Télégraphique and Téléphonique (PTT)   The Poste Télégraphique and Téléphonique, PTT, is a national quasi-govern-

Swiss Telecom is typical of most PTTs' shift away from restrictiveness, toward liberalization and service. In 1989, a Switzerland to New York leased line cost 10 times as much as one from New York to Switzerland. Now the PTT is investing $10 billion over the next three years to position itself as a hub for European communications. Rates for leased circuits were slashed by 30–40 percent in April 1991.

mental agency responsible for telecommunications. Historically, PTTs have tried to control business exploitation of emerging technical advances in telecommunications in order to preserve their own revenues. This highly restrictive environment is rapidly breaking down as PTTs around the world liberalize, deregulate, and even privatize at varied rates and with varied degrees of enthusiasm.

See also: International Telecommunications, Public Data Network

Private Network   The private/public network distinction can be misleading inasmuch as both are typically provided by a telecommunications supplier such as AT&T, MCI, or US Sprint in the United States, British Telecom or Mercury in Great Britain, and PTTs elsewhere in the world. The difference is that a private network is a fixed-cost capability leased from the telecommunications provider, which guarantees levels of capacity and performance, whereas a public network provides a general access, pay-as-you-go service.

The advantage of a private network is that it allows a company with skilled communications professionals to manage its communications traffic more efficiently. The user has no control over traffic on a public network, and no way to ensure a given service level or security. Virtual private networks, a variant on private networks, offer many cost advantages for large firms. The provider of a virtual private network guarantees a contracted level of service without providing dedicated facilities.

The providers of public data networks have an immense advantage of scale. They are upgrading their systems rapidly with advanced technology, particularly fiber optics, to lower costs and improve performance. During the 1980s, the cost, security, and quality trade-offs between private and public networks led large firms to favor private networks for their high-volume processing and communications systems. The choice is less clear now, and the distinction between private and public networks is blurring as the top providers offer a growing range of options to small and large businesses alike.

See also: International Telecommunications, Network, Telecommunications, Transmission, Value-Added Network

Programming Programming is the process of transforming a description of a system design into instructions that can be interpreted by a computer. Ultimately, these instructions must be specified in the form of the binary coding (0–1) that is used to represent the electrical states stored in the circuits of computer chips. Because binary coding is extrordinarily tedious and time-consuming, multiple levels of programming "languages" have evolved, each with its own vocabulary and rules of grammar. The link between the application programs written in higher-level languages and what occurs in the circuits of the computer is provided by compilers, translation software supplied by the hardware vendor.

Application programming languages include BASIC, FORTRAN (which is particularly well suited to developing scientific applications), COBOL (long the standard for business applications), Ada (the required language for Department of Defense systems development) and newer, higher-level languages called fourth-generation languages, or 4GLs, which permit users to do a considerable amount of application development on their own.

Everything that happens in a computer has been programmed. The operating systems that perform all the utilitarian but absolutely essential operational tasks, including reading application programs and data into memory, performing the required processing, and seeing that everything is properly stored when it is finished are written by systems programmers. Applications, both custom applications commissioned for specific tasks and the many general purpose packages developed to support generic applications are written by teams of programmers. The growing use of very high-level languages, such as 4GLs, which hide the complexity of the programming task to enable users to do some of their own programming, is consistent with other trends, such as distributed computing, networking, and the client/server model of computing that put more responsibility on the user.

See also: *Application Software and Application Development, Computer-Aided Software Engineering, End-User Computing, Object-Oriented Programming, Operating System, Prototyping, Systems Programming*

The typical U.S. business application program has 4.4 bugs per thousand lines of program code that will be located in the first twelve months of use. The equivalent Japanese program has just under two.

Proprietary   Proprietary refers to products that are specific to a single vendor. In practice, much proprietary software becomes, de facto, "open" as other vendors build products that are compatible with it. An example is IBM's MS.DOS operating system for its personal computers. Conversely, many implementations of open systems are rendered proprietary in practice by the addition of special features. Although the two industry leaders in computers, IBM and DEC, develop proprietary products, both are fully committed to ensuring that their systems comply with market-driven and market-proven open systems and standards.

See also: Compatibility, MS.DOS, Open Systems, Operating System, OS/2, Standards, Systems Integration, UNIX

Protocol   A protocol is a procedure for establishing a telecommunications link. Indeed, protocols are the language of telecommunications interconnection. They reflect many aspects of protocols in the diplomatic sense, the signals exchanged by sending and receiving devices, for example, being termed "handshaking" and "acknowledgment."

Protocols are primarily concerned with three aspects of the communication process: how data are represented and coded; how data are transmitted; and how errors and failures are recognized and handled. Much of the incompatibility between telecommunications facilities relates to the use of different protocols and much of the discussion of telecommunications standards centers around protocols. Open standards, gateways, bridges, and protocol converters all address incompatibility in different ways and with varying degrees of effectiveness.

See also: Compatibility, Interface, Network, Packet-Switching, Proprietary, Standards, Telecommunications, Transmission

Prototyping   Prototyping refers to the process of building a small working version of a systems design as a means of hedging risk, encouraging experiment, and fueling learning. The use of prototyping to get a clearer idea of user needs is a surprisingly recent innovation. Early systems development techniques, which focused on automating clerical procedures to improve efficiency, relied on well-defined design specifications, often running to many hundreds of pages. Changing a design once it had become the base for a set of software programs, together with the inherent and continuing complexity of systems development, testing, and operation presented major difficulties.

In retrospect, it is apparent that reliance on functional specifications and detailed design at the start of a major project increased risks. Users could not know what they wanted, having little if any experience with computers, and the technology was inflexible and experimentation impractical, making development an all-or-nothing endeavor. A system worked or it did not, but it took two to five years to find out.

IT is increasingly being applied to business activities for which no written set of procedures exist. As emphasis has shifted from automating processes to supporting how people work, ensuring ease of use, flexibility, and adaptability have become key design requirements. In helping to satisfy these requirements, prototyping has become for systems developers what wind tunnel models are for bridge builders and "breadboarded" systems for systems engineers.

Care must be taken to ensure that prototyping does not become a substitute for systematic analysis. Imagine a bridge builder saying, "I have no idea what we need, let's knock up a prototype," then building some models and concluding, "OK, that looks right. Let's build it." Prototyping is a systematic discipline; it should not be a substitute for planning. Too often a prototype, instead of being thrown away and the learning gained from it used to ensure a first-rate design, becomes the base for the full design.

Prototyping is a powerful vehicle for bringing designers and users together, allowing designers to get a sense of how a system is intended to work, and enabling users to evolve their stated needs by using a real system. A sound prototype is the best evidence that a proposed design is likely to work, both organizationally and technically.

See also: *Application Software and Application Development, Computer-Aided Software Engineering, Programming, Testing*

No construction firm would build a bridge without first designing and testing a model. Information systems designers did the equivalent of that for decades until the tools of computer terminals, time-sharing, personal computers, fourth-generation languages, and the like made it practical to design a system by starting from a prototype and learning by using.

PTT   See Poste Télégraphique and Téléphonique

More and more commentators are concerned that the United States lacks a coherent policy for ensuring that the country has a comprehensive public network capability to match that of almost all other countries.

Public Data Network (PDN)   A public data network, or PDN, is a telecommunications system that anyone can subscribe to and use on an as-needed basis. As with the public voice network, the telephone system the tariff for a PDN is volume-sensitive. Users pay as they go; the more traffic they put through the network, the more they pay. In many countries, public data networks are the only available option for businesses, private networks being either unavailable or prohibitively expensive.

See also: International Telecommunications, Network, Poste Télégraphique and Téléphonique, Private Network, Telecommuncations

RAM   See Random Access Memory

Random Access Memory   Computer memory is called "random access" because the central processing unit can directly access any part of it to retrieve and store information and the time required to do so is independent of the location of the information previously accessed. This contrasts with magnetic tape storage, which must be accessed sequentially.

See also: CD-ROM, Central Processing Unit, Chip, Disk Storage, Image Technology, Millisecond, Response Time

RBOC   See Regional Bell Operating Company

Read Only Memory (ROM)   Read only memory, or ROM, is a computer chip that stores data or instructions in a form that cannot be altered. It is contrasted with random access memory (RAM), the contents of which can be changed. The contents of a ROM chip, unlike those of a RAM chip are not lost when power is shut off to the computer. There are several variants of ROM, including programmable ROM (PROM) and electrically erasable programmable ROM (EEPROM).

ROM chips are widely used to store computer game programs and to store the operating system and application programs for some laptop computers. Automobile engines contain ROM chips that control many functions.

See also: Chip, Random Access Memory

Recovery   See Backup and Recovery

Reduced Instruction Set Computing (RISC)   Reduced instruction set computing, or RISC, is a type of chip logic that contains electronic circuits that provide a very limited number of computer instructions (for multiplication, addition, comparing values, and so forth). Most application programs use only a few instructions for almost all their processing. RISC technology exploits this fact by providing only a small set of instructions that execute very quickly. Because they are less expensive to produce than general purpose logic chips, RISC chips are the basis for many of the powerful new workstations that provide computing power at very low cost.

RISC technology is not suited to all types of applications. So far, it has been used for functions that require raw computation speed but do not involve complex information handling.

See also: *Central Processing Unit, Chip*

It is ironic that simplifying computer chips and eliminating many of their most powerful instruction capabilities has led to dramatic increases in the overall power of workstations. RISC technology is the base for all the leading UNIX workstations, and has increased their price-performance by factors of twenty in two years.

Regional Bell Operating Company (RBOC)   The Regional Bell Operating Companies, the "Baby Bells" created by the divestiture of AT&T in 1984, today hold considerable power in the telecommunications industry through their control of the local access points to long-distance services, although they are constrained from entering many potentially profitable markets in information services. The substantial revenues of the seven RBOCs (Ameritech, Bell Atlantic, BellSouth, NYNEX, Pacific Telesis, Southwestern Bell, and US West) thus come mainly from the provision of basic telephone services. NYNEX, for example, derives 85 percent of its $13 billion in annual sales from local telephone service. But with voice traffic growing at only 3–5 percent per year in revenues (the figure is 7 percent in volume, technology and competition in long-distance markets having driven revenue per unit down) and data communications at 15–30 percent per year (depending on type of traffic and industry), the RBOCs face a flattening revenue base. Consequently, they periodically petition the courts to allow them to expand their services, and meanwhile have begun to buy into foreign joint ventures — even foreign PTTs, as they are deregulated and privatized. BellSouth, for example, wholly owns a European paging company, and US West is implementing Hungary's first cellular system and is part owner of U.K. Cable Corporation, the largest cable firm in the English-speaking world.

See also: Cellular Communication, International Telecommunications, Mobile Communication, Network

Until recently, most data bases were organized "hierarchically," rather analogous to the filing hierarchy of cabinet, drawer, folder, document, and item within the document. A relational data base indexes and cross-references data at the item level.

Relational Data Base   A relational data base is organized so that its contents can be cross referenced. A major area of development in computer science, software, and business applications, the relational data base is a deceptively simple concept that is immensely complex to implement technically and organizationally. It involves entirely new types of software and extremely heavy overhead in processing and operations. Despite unsolved problems in many areas of high volume, RDBMs are a key element in creating organizational data resources that can be classified, analyzed, and accessed as if they were part of the indexed contents of an enormous library.

See also: Data, Data-Base Management System

Response Time   The quality of a system from a user's perspective is strongly dependent on response time, the time it takes the system to respond to a request. Network managers and designers of on-line services set response time as a service measure, aiming at X seconds response in Y percent of cases, typically, 3–5 seconds in 95 percent of transactions. Heavy traffic on a network or a large number of transactions accessing the same software or data base can quickly degrade response time. Few business applications require single-second response time (the response time of human beings is much slower as they reflect and make their next choice), but when response time approaches 15 seconds user patience begins to be taxed.

See also: Automated Teller Machine, Computerized Reservation System, Electronic Funds Transfer at Point Of Sale, On-Line Transaction Processing, Terminal, User

RISC   See Reduced Instruction Set Computing

ROM   See Read Only Memory

Router   See Bridges, Routers, and Gateways

Satellite   Communication satellites move in a geosynchronous orbit 22,300 miles above the earth, which makes them stationary from the perspective of terrestrial facilities. Information is transmitted as very high-frequency radio signals (in the gigahertz range) to a satellite's transponder, which boosts the signals and transmits them back down to any receiving antenna within its broadcast range (termed its footprint). Satellites are used by television stations to broadcast programming to millions of television sets and by businesses to broadcast data bases, training programs, management reviews, and product announcements to any number of offices and personal computers. Ground stations can also initiate transactions, which are routed by satellite to a central computer.

Satellite transmission has two advantages over "terrestrial" transmission: (1) the costs are the same whether there are two or two million downlinks receiving the information being broadcast, and (2) they do not require massive infrastructure investments in cables. This makes them particularly well suited to serving the communications needs of countries such as India and Indonesia, in which the principal business, government, and university centers are separated by vast distances. A disadvantage of satellite communication is the "propagation" delay of one-quarter second, the time it takes a transmission to make the nearly 50,000-mile round trip.

The international satellite market is intensely political and dominated by one organization, Intelsat, which is jointly owned by 114 countries. U.S. telecommunications providers were required from the 1960s until the 1980s to send a large proportion of their international traffic over Intelsat's 13 satellites. Satellite communication will face greater competition as the economies of fiber optics, which also provides massive bandwidth, become more attractive.

See also: Bandwidth, Business Television, International Telecommunications, Megahertz, Mobile Communication, Telecommunications, Transmission, Videoconferencing, Very Small Aperture Terminal

Scanner   See Image Technology

The main advantages of satellites over "terrestrial" transmission are they do not need an expensive investment in a national infrastructure, and they can be used for broadcasting data; adding another earth station receiver does not add any transmission cost. Countries like Indonesia and India could not possibly afford to install fiber optics across their broad geographic spread. A third advantage, of course, is that satellites can send messages to ships at sea and airplanes in flight.

Security   All electronic services face a conflict between access and control. The purpose of ATMs, electronic mail, and on-line information systems is to provide easy and convenient access to information, which makes control of that information difficult.

Passwords are a means of restricting access to information to authorized users. They are a primitive form of security that can generally be broken by skilled hackers. Encryption is a technique for scrambling information to make it unintelligible during transmission. Encryption can add another level of protection to passwords by preventing an accidental intruder, hacker, or computer criminal who gains access to information from making any sense of it. An emerging strategy of large financial services and telecommunications companies is to develop expert systems that scan for patterns of activity that suggest misuse. Network management software is also providing more in the way of "sentinel" facilities, audit controls, and so forth.

The central dilemma concerning security is that it is close to impossible to provide both open access and control. Our on-line systems are being built to provide access to more and more people. The telephone is the most vulnerable system, with calling card fraud costing consumers $500 million a year, according to the FCC; the figure for business losses is surely several times that.

Security is a time bomb. Many of today's IT systems are about as secure as alarms and locks on Porsches in New York City; they deter amateurs but are easy for professionals to break into. On-line services are particularly vulnerable to deliberate attacks on security and credit card fraud, telephone calling card, and ATM thefts run into many billions of dollars per year.

Most surveys of security issues emphasize that negligence and incompetence are greater problems than computer hackers, criminals, or "viruses" (hidden programs introduced into a computer system for the purpose of damaging other programs and data files). The biggest single impediment to ensuring security is business management's lack of real interest in the topic. Many companies have no effective protection against accidental loss of service, deliberate intrusion, and sustained efforts to steal information and money electronically.

See also: *Architecture, Backup and Recovery, Encryption, Mobile Communication, Network, Virus*

Shell   See Artificial Intelligence

Smart Card   Often thought of as a credit card with an embedded computer chip, a smart card is, in effect, a personal computer in a wallet. To date, there have been only scattered applications of the smart card, but many commentators see a wide range of opportunities in a device that contains enough memory to store records and handle transactions without the need for telecommunications links to remote facilities.

Every year, articles appear in the IT press that announce that this really will be the year of the smart card. We have yet to see it. Smart cards are a solution searching for the right problem. There have been many successful small-scale applications but no single blockbuster application capable of moving smart cards into the mainstream of business and consumer use.

A smart card is effectively a key that is inserted into a workstation, pay phone, ATM, or other access point to obtain IT-based services. The card's memory stores profile information, can update balances, and incorporates security features.

The Royal Bank of Canada uses smart cards to control access to its cash management services. The cards contain a portion of the program instructions for cash management transaction processing and an encryption feature that scrambles the transaction information. The system will work only if the smart card is on-line at the cash management workstation.

Pay telephones in France have for several years accepted smart cards that store a prepaid amount of money. The cost of a call is deducted from the amount remaining on the card. Many observers see such debit cards as the principal long-term opportunity for smart cards.

The most extensive application of smart card technology to date in the United States is the Department of Agriculture's program for managing government-supported quotas for peanut growers. Each farmer in the program is provided with a smart card containing agreed-on quota and price information. As farmers sell their crops, sale amounts are deducted from the quotas on their cards and the transactions are approved and processed directly on the basis of the stored card data. The system has cut the time needed to complete the processing of crop sales from two weeks to less than 15 minutes.

See also: *Chip, Encryption, Security*

The smart card is really a personal computer in the wallet. Although the successes are scattered and every prediction that this will be "the year of the smart card" gets rolled forward another year, the Japanese car industry seems to be providing the push that creates a critical mass. A smart card comes with the car, and is used to store the car's service and repair history.

Socket   See Cables, Plugs, and Sockets

Software   Software is what gives hardware functionality. There are three major classes of software. Systems software handles operating system and related functions that provide the facilities for application software to run efficiently. Customized application software for specific business functions is developed by business analysts and programmers. Application software packages, designed to serve more generic needs, often must be modified to meet company-specific requirements.

If only software productivity could keep pace with the improvement in hardware and telecommunications! Software is the driver of business innovation through IT, the bottleneck to exploiting hardware, the main cost and risk element, and increasingly the determinant of customer service and quality.

Customized application software development is expensive and a major bottleneck in many firms. Software productivity has not kept pace with improvements in the cost-effectiveness of hardware, largely because, being intellectually difficult to master, manage, maintain, and document, it is dependent on skilled and experienced human staff. Computer systems are typically replaced every two years by faster, less-expensive, and more powerful systems, but the software that runs on them may be several decades old.

Software and services account for more than half of the worldwide $300-billion computer industry. One multinational firm calculates that it has in use today more than 30,000 programs with 70 million lines of code that cost more than $1 billion to create and that would require $3–7 billion to replicate. This is not unusual. Because software development is expensed (the major cost is salaries), it does not appear on firms' balance sheets. Many *Fortune* 1000 firms have spent a billion dollars or more to create software and do not know it. If they did, senior management might recognize that software is a major capital asset that should be managed as such, and devote more time and attention to it.

See also: *Application Software and Application Development, Computer-Aided Software Engineering, Programming, Prototyping, Systems Programming, Testing*

Spreadsheet   See Software

SQL   See Structured Query Language

Standards Standards are agreements on formats, procedures, and interfaces that permit designers of hardware, software, data bases, and telecommunications facilities to develop products and systems independent of one another with the assurance that they will be compatible with any other product or system that adheres to the same standards. They are the single most important element in achieving integration of the corporate information and communications resource.

The standard-setting process — because it involves negotiations among IT providers and users, formal agreements and definitions, certification and testing procedures, and documentation and publication — can be extraordinarily cumbersome and lengthy. It can take more than a decade to complete the process of defining a standard and implementing it in commercial products.

A recent report identified nearly 50 committees and organizations involved in setting standards for international telecommunications. It should not be surprising that the work of so many different entities often overlaps and conflicts. Literally thousands of standards exist for the principal elements of information technology. Being voluntary, these standards have no legal weight, hence they are not enforceable except as government agencies and companies mandate compliance with particular standards as a precondition for bidding on contracts.

Committee-based organizations such as the American National Standards Institute (ANSI) and its international equivalents, the International Standards Organization (ISO) and Consultative Committee for International Telephony and Telegraphy (CCITT), have historically dominated the standard-setting process. But because technology is today evolving too fast for the slow, debate-oriented and often contention-ridden committee process (which tends to be dominated by academics, vendors, and the largely quasi-government national telecommunications providers), computer and telecommunications vendors and leading users and industry groups are playing a growing role both in defining standards and influencing their adoption in the marketplace. Examples include the U.S. Department of Defense, which defined its own standard for programming languages and established a list of requirements that contractors must follow, and the

U.S. grocery and transportation and European automotive industries (among others), which have established electronic data interchange standards to govern intercompany transactions.

Standards establish the pace for what is practical for business, yet many leading U.S. companies are unfamiliar with the standard-setting process and the industry groups that coordinate and try to influence it. Individual businesses are now beginning to take a more active role. A group nicknamed the Houston 30, for example, established the User Alliance for Open Systems, and vendors and users alike have joined organizations such as the Open Systems Foundation and the Corporation for Open Systems.

To remedy heretofore weak representation in the standard-setting process, U.S. companies should encourage senior Information Services staff to participate actively in user and industry standards groups. The perspectives and priorities of business users are often very different from those of the national telecommunications authorities and computer vendors that have historically dominated the standard-setting process. Business must drive what is increasingly a business issue.

Some of the more prominent standards relevant to the design of a firm's information systems architecture are described briefly below. Those elaborated more fully in separate entries are listed in the "see also" reference.

FDDI, a key standard for high-speed fiber optic local area networks, is expected to become the base standard for the networks of the 1990s. Current costs of implementation are fairly high, but the standard's potential for increasing telecommunications speed and capability is immense.

ISDN is the long-defined, slow to be implemented, and, to date, apathetically received blueprint for enabling the world's public telephone systems to convey information of all types — including voice, image, and data — cheaply and efficiently, in digital form, through a universal telephone jack.

EDIFACT, the leading standard for international electronic data interchange, includes procedures for defining trade- and industry-specific EDI standards. To date, EDIFACT has generated more than 50 message sets that cover the most important and common types of international transactions in trade, transport, banking, insurance, customs, construction, and tourism.

Ethernet, a local area network standard initially developed by Xerox, is today widely implemented in commercial products. Ethernet is particularly well suited to connecting workstations and departmental computers that traffic heavily in messages that are brief and intermittent.

OSI (Open Systems Interconnection) is a blueprint for resolving problems of incompatibility. It creates a "reference model" that allows designers of telecommunications networks and networking equipment to develop products and services that are able to interconnect independently of the technology used. OSI establishes interfaces at seven levels: the lowest governs physical interconnections; the highest, interconnections between applications.

X12 is the principal domestic technical standard for electronic data interchange. It is closely related to EDIFACT, and the basis for most industry cooperative agreements on standards for EDI transactions.

X.25 is the principal standard for public data networks and international telecommunications. It is by far the best-established standard for wide area networks. Newer standards, notably frame relay, are extending X.25 to take advantage of tremendous improvements in reliability and speed of transmission since X.25 was defined in the 1970s.

X.400 is an important emerging standard for all forms of electronic messaging, including electronic mail, telex, and fax. Defined in 1984, X.400 began to be widely implemented by leading electronic mail service and software providers in the early 1990s.

X.500 is an emerging standard that defines electronic network directories for purposes of allowing devices on different networks to locate one another. Thus it will provide a basis for automatic linkages across international networks, an impossibility today.

IEEE 802.1, 802.2...802.5 are standards for local area networks

Standards have become the core of the IT industry, organizations' IT planning, vendor strategies, and national and international telecommunications policy.

defined by the Institute of Electrical and Electronic Engineers (IEEE). Key standards from a business perspective are 802.3 (Ethernet) and 802.5 (Token Ring).

See also: ANSI, Architecture, ASCII, Compatible, Consultative Committee for International Telephony and Telegraphy, EDIFACT, Electronic Data Interchange, Encryption, Ethernet, Fiber Distributed Data Interface,Integrated Services Digital Network, Integration, Interface, Network, Open Systems Interconnection, Platform, Token Ring, X12, X.25, X.400, X.500

Structured Query Language (SQL)   Structured Query Language, or SQL, has become the standard interface for relational data-base management systems, including those that run on personal computers. It enables a user to access information without knowing where it is located or how it is structured. SQL is easier to use than a programming language but more complex than spreadsheet or word processing software. A simple SQL statement may generate a set of requests for information stored on different computers in scattered locations, and hence consume a significant amount of time and computing resources. SQL can be used for interactive inquiries or ad hoc report generation or embedded in application programs.

See also: Data, Relational Data Base

Supercomputer   Supercomputers are ultra high-speed "number crunchers" used primarily for scientific and engineering applications. These include weather forecasting that involves masses of calculations. The new generation of supercomputers differs from conventional mainframe computers in its use of parallel processing. A business computer processes instructions one at a time in a single CPU. Parallel processing involves the use of up to thousands of small CPUs to simultaneously process the parts of a mathematical task that has been broken down into many subtasks. The difference is like asking someone to find all the names in a telephone directory for which the first name is "James." A conventional computer would begin at "A" and move page by page through "Z." A parallel processing machine would assign page 1 to microprocessor 1, page 2 to processor 2, and so on.

The hardware, operating systems, and application software for

Prudential Securities found that running a critical and very time-dependent analysis on its mainframe computer would take 16,000 minutes, or 11 days. A Cray supercomputer would cut that to 100 minutes. A cluster of supercomputers handles the analysis in 30–120 seconds. Programming supercomputers, which increasingly link a number of machines for "massively parallel processing;" is as different from writing business applications as French is from Italian.

supercomputers are entirely different from those for standard business computers. Most companies will never need a supercomputer. But computer-aided design in manufacturing, microeconomic analysis, bond pricing in the securities industry, and even animation for films are moving supercomputers out of the lab. Parallel processing may be a major direction for handling very large-scale data bases.

See also: Computer-Aided Design/Computer-Aided Manufacturing, Mainframe and Minicomputer

Switch Telecommunications transmission relies on techniques for sharing a high-speed link among many slower devices and routing messages through a network along the most efficient transmission path. Switch is a generic term for the hardware that manages the traffic routing and transmission. These devices include multiplexers, PBX (private branch exchange) and ISDN switches, and such related devices as cluster controllers, X.25 PADs (packet assemblers/disassemblers), and ACDs (automatic call distributors).

Switches coordinate and synchronize the operations of a network. They are very expensive and their selection, implementation, and operation demand highly specialized technical expertise. One of the key factors influencing a firm's choice of private versus public networks and in-house operations versus outsourcing is the capital cost and skill base needed to manage an advanced telecommunications network. Having someone else handle the complexities of the technology may be a sensible choice for many firms, but others feel that they can achieve a comparative cost or even competitive advantage by designing and managing their own networks.

See also: Network, Network Management, Telecommunications

Synchronous Optical Network (SONET) See Bandwidth, Fiber Optics

Systems Development See Application Software and Application Development

Systems Integration Systems integration refers to providing a technical solution to a business need that involves fitting together the relevant technical components. These generally include existing incompatible hardware, software, and data bases as well as new systems. The rapid growth of the systems integration market reflects the degree of systems disintegration in most large firms. Incompatible systems have become a blockage to business effectiveness by preventing the cross-linking of services and sharing of information and communication networks.

The systems integrators that deliver fully integrated systems of software, hardware, and telecommunications are an outgrowth of the systems development contractors of the 1980s that built software systems for client firms' mainframe computers. Systems integration is thus neither new nor special. What is new is the growth of a small number of firms competing to establish themselves as leaders in a fast-growing and very large market. The Big Eight accounting firms (down to six following several mergers) saw early the opportunity to add systems integration to their auditing and consulting base. Andersen Consulting, an offshoot of Arthur Andersen and Company, is the third-largest single systems integrator, behind IBM and EDS. Major computer vendors, including IBM and Digital Equipment Corporation, seeing systems integration as a priority market, are accepting that they must be able to provide skills in other vendors' products as well as their own.

The systems integration market is growing at 20 percent a year, mainly because there is so much existing systems disintegration.

The systems integration market is growing at close to 20 percent per year, far faster than the overall IT market, primarily because firms have neither the skills nor the spare development staff to handle the often massive projects they need to undertake to position themselves for the business context of the 1990s. Information Systems units are increasingly multisourcing their development, handling some in-house, contracting some out to systems integrators, handling some through joint ventures, often with firms that have already implemented the main base for a system they can use and outsourcing some operations for fixed annual fees.

The reality of applications development has always been that demand exceeds supply of skilled staff. As long as business needs drive the demand for integrated systems to meet the demands of cross-functional business coordination and development, the systems integration market will continue to expand.

See also: Architecture, Compatibility, Integration, Open Systems, Platform

Systems Life Cycle Systems life cycle refers to the sequence of steps from the inception of a new application to its eventual termination and replacement. The main phases and the amount of development time they should take are planning and design, 40 percent; program coding, 10 percent; testing, 30 percent; and installation, 20 percent. In the five years after development, maintenance and operations will amount to from 100–300 percent of the original development cost. Exact percentages will vary, of course, depending on the type of application, but these numbers should hold for most large-scale application development projects.

The most important point to note is that programming represents just 10 percent of total development effort. Testing, by comparison, accounts for three times as much time and effort. In the early days of application development, programming was the main focus of planning and budgeting. The new profession was, after all, called computer "programming." But over time it became apparent that this focus was totally inappropriate. A complex system requires very detailed planning, and design issues must address ease of use and flexibility. Furthermore, specifications must be checked and rechecked, since the cost of correcting errors is greater the later into the development process they are discovered. An error that costs $1 to correct in the planning and design stage will cost $10 to correct in the programming stage, $100 in the testing stage, and $1,000 after the system is operational.

The length of time major systems development projects take can be very frustrating for business managers who need them operational as soon as possible. But pressures to cut corners and speed projects up generally end up adding to the cost in the long run. Bugs that are not located in the testing process will turn up when they will not only be more expensive to correct, but when they may damage customer service and operations.

Most of the costs of a software system are incurred after it is developed. Every $1 of development typically generates 20 cents of operations and 40 cents of maintenance. The original $1 expense is really $4 of capital over a five-year period.

Systems Programming   Systems programmers are technical specialists in some aspect of operating systems, data-base management systems, or telecommunications network software. These are the technical wizards whose job is to ensure efficient operation of the overall IT resource. Their knowledge is generally highly specific in terms of vendors and operating systems, and most have a strong computer science background and little interest in the business issues that concern applications programmers.

Systems programmers play a critical role in firms whose cash flow depends on the quality of their IT operations. When a bank's ATM network is down, so is the bank. With the emphasis in Information Systems departments on being service- and business-oriented and bridging the historical culture and attitude gaps between IS and its business users, there is a tendency for "techies" to be dismissed or even disdained. But the more complex a firm's IT base and the more critical it is to business operations, the more vital it is that the firm have access to the best systems specialists.

Skilled systems programmers and their equivalents in telecommunications are becoming harder to find, reflecting a nearly one-third decline in enrollments in computer science in U.S. universities in the past five years. Meanwhile the technology continues to develop at a dizzying pace, making it hard for experienced systems programmers to keep up-to-date in their field.

See also: Computer-Aided Software Engineering, Network Management, Operating System, Programming

Telecommunications   Telecommunications is the electronic movement of information. Telecommunications used to imply telephones, telex, and a much slower and more expensive facsimile than we are familiar with today. A rough rule of thumb that held through the mid-1970s was that voice accounted for 85 percent of a company's communications traffic. The remainder, largely digital data generated by computers, was distinguished as "data communications," and had to be converted to analog form by a device called a modem before being transmitted over the telephone network, often using leased lines specially conditioned for data traffic.

Today, the proportions are reversing. Data communications traffic generated by computers has become a key element in business operations and telecommunications providers are scrambling to convert the communications infrastructure to digital and evolve standards that will accommodate the simultaneous transmission of voice and data traffic over the same lines. (This is being done to a limited extent today.)

Until recently, telecommunications has embodied a separate set of skills and experience and been a separate organizational unit from Information Systems. Few heads of IS have come up through the telecommunications field, which, until the late 1980s, tended to be a specialist area heavily focused on the highly complex technical details of telecommunications operations, with little emphasis on business planning and information systems strategies.

Changing this situation is becoming a priority for many organizations as the perception of telecommunications shifts from that of a support technology to that of an infrastructure technology that provides a base, or platform, for computing applications. Most major issues in standards, integration, and architecture center around telecommunications; networking, rather than computing, now drives most major initiatives in the business deployment of information technology.

Telecommunications is a major political issue internationally, since in every country except the United States it has historically been run by a quasi-government monopoly that did not permit competition. Thus companies have had little choice in telecommunications, and prices and use have been highly regulated. The trend toward liberalization in telecommunications is well established today. Liberalization permits limited competition and choice, but retains monopoly regulation. Some countries have entirely deregulated or even privatized their PTTs.

See also: *Architecture, Backbone Network, International Telecommunications, Network, Network Management, Platform, Standards, Terminal, Transmission*

Telecommunications eliminates barriers of geography and time on coordination, service, logistics, communication, and physical location. It has become key to how firms compete, how cities compete, and how economies grow. Unfortunately, relatively few business or IS managers or computer professionals are familiar with telecommunications, and the telecommunications profession has largely focused so heavily on details of operations and equipment that it has not built an effective dialogue with IS, let alone business. Where there is such a dialogue, there is immense opportunity for competitive and organizational innovation.

Teller Machine   See Automated Teller Machine

Terminal   Computer terminals first allowed flexible, occasional, ad hoc access to central information stores and "time-shared" computer processing. Early computers processed work sequentially, one task at a time. Time-sharing divided a computer's processing among many tasks simultaneously, and computer terminals provided a way to submit work remotely, from locations physically removed from the computer. Except when the location was close enough to be cabled directly to the computer, the connection was usually established over telephone lines using a modem. Early terminals were typewriter-like devices; later terminals incorporated video displays, giving them much the same appearance as today's personal computers. Terminals are distinguished from PCs in that they can do no processing independently of their connection to a computer. (Exceptions were so-called "smart terminals" that possessed some storage or limited processing capability; they constitute an intermediate stage in the evolution of the personal computer.) Time sharing began to run into trouble when the number of terminals competing for a computer's time became so great that the computer's response time was degraded.

See also: Data Center, Mainframe and Minicomputer, On-Line Transaction Processing, Personal Computer, Response Time, Telecommunications

Testing   Any large-scale application system will inevitably contain errors, or "bugs," as they are known in the trade. The testing phase of development aims at finding as many bugs as possible before a system is released. But even with the most rigorous testing, at least four errors per thousand lines of code will typically be found in an operational system during its first 12 months of use.

Testing is done primarily by running sample transactions — routine transactions, special cases, and deliberate mistakes — through the system in a systematic manner. Programmers can check the logic of a program to ensure that calculations are made according to the design specifications, but only people who are familiar with the business and work context can spot output that looks correct but is not, or can anticipate unusual but occasional combinations of inputs that need to be tested. Testing a system generally takes three times as much time and effort as writing the program code.

Testing is boring. It is vital. Systems developers have elaborate test plans and procedures. Most users of spreadsheets on PCs do not have test plans and procedures. Have you ever made or approved a decision based on a spreadsheet? Did you ask how it was tested?

There is no substitute for testing. Professional programmers are well aware of the need for it and of the arcane and tiny bugs that can crash a program. Personal computer users may not be so sensitive to the fact that even the simplest spreadsheet may contain bugs and that it needs careful testing.

See also: Application Software and Application Development, Bugs, Maintenance, Programming, Systems Life Cycle

Token Ring
The Token Ring standard was an important development in the evolution of local area networking and constitutes the principal rival to the popular Ethernet standard. Token Ring is the basis for IBM local area networks and their integration into wide area networks.

See also: Ethernet, Local Area Network, Network, Standards

Transmission
Transmission refers to the movement of information through a telecommunications network. It is concerned with establishing links over which to send information and ensuring that it arrives accurately and reliably. The medium used to create the path between the sending and receiving device may be some type of physical cable or through-the-air radio signal. Copper cable, fiber optics, satellite, and microwave are all equivalent in that each provides the means to carry a signal.

Transmission links may be point-to-point, which means that a single device links to another single device as in a telephone call, or point-to-multipoint, in which one sender transmits to many receivers, as in broadcast television.

Transmission speeds are measured in bits per second (bps). Dial-up telephone lines typically operate at speeds of up to 9,600 bps. The fiber optic links that are expected to be the base of the networks of the mid-1990s will provide speeds in excess of two billion bps (2 Gbps). These high-speed transmission links will be shared among many simultaneous users through techniques called multiplexing. One related technique, called packet-switching, is the basis for most international public data networks that use the X.25 technical standard

Telecommunications providers such as MCI, AT&T, and foreign PTTs have mainly focused on transmission—moving bits from sender to receiver. They were not interested in the nature of those bits and of the applications they were part of. There is a widespread feeling among most IS and business managers that they need to broaden their thinking and their services.

designed to provide low-cost transmission to thousands of users at the cost of some loss of efficiency in throughput.

See also: Cables, Plugs, and Sockets, Cellular Communication, Connectivity, Digital, Encryption, Fiber Optics, International Telecommunications, Megahertz, Mobile Communication, Modem, Network, Packet-Switching, Protocol, Regional Bell Operating Companies, Response Time, Satellite, Security, Standards, Switch, Telecommunications

UNIX   UNIX is an operating system, a religion, a political movement, and a mass of committees. It has been a favorite operating system of technical experts for many years owing to its "portability" across different operating environments and hardware, its support of "multitasking" (running a number of different programs at the same time), and its building-block philosophy of systems development (building libraries of small "blocks" from which complex systems can be built).

UNIX was developed in the early 1970s by Bell Labs, which licensed it for general use. Recently, UNIX has moved out of specialized scientific and academic environments. It has become very popular in engineering and manufacturing.

Proponents see UNIX as providing four distinctive advantages. One is its design for maximum practical vendor-independence and portability across machines, which makes it a potential cornerstone for truly open systems. Two, it exploits the many developments in hardware and communications that have marked the past decade better than proprietary operating systems that have had to ensure that old software could continue to be run, however inefficiently, on newer hardware. Three, its strength in "multitasking," or running a number of applications concurrently at a single workstation, makes it the best available choice for client/server computing. And four, its Lego-block philosophy of developing small units of code that can be combined and shared has resulted in the compilation of rich libraries of routines.

Although technically an "open" system, there are many varieties of UNIX, and the two leading vendor consortia trying to develop a single version are in open conflict. The UNIX International Group comprises the old guard of UNIX, developer AT&T, and the companies that have been committed to it through the 1980s. The Open Software Foundation includes recent converts to UNIX such as IBM and Digital Equipment Corporation. The core of the latter's UNIX standard includes additional features that make it essentially competitive and incompatible with the other group's standard.

Because vendors naturally add functions to differentiate their versions, UNIX has become an example of a standard that is open in definition but, to date at least, proprietary in implementation. MS.DOS, by contrast, is proprietary in definition but open in implementation.

Many Information Services managers, for whom the commonalities in UNIX implementations far outweigh the differences, see UNIX as the cutting edge of information technology. Others are more circumspect. A frequent criticism of UNIX is that it is basically geared to technical applications, reflecting its origins at Bell Labs and its strong history of university use and development. Skeptics, pointing to a lack of applications and of development staff experienced in commercial applications, doubt that it will be either useful nor practical to move existing systems onto a UNIX platform. It will be at least five years before we know if UNIX is just another niche in the broader IT field or a key driving force. The federal government's commitment to Posix (portable operating system interface for UNIX) guarantees sustained momentum and a large market, as does the growing number of computer vendors that staked their futures on UNIX, partly because the top two manufacturers, IBM and DEC, were holding out.

Now that IBM has provided a powerful set of workstations based on its own version of UNIX and leading UNIX providers have developed linkages with IBM's main operating systems and telecommunications architectures, UNIX is positioned to be part of a firm's architecture. The religious wars can end and peaceful coexistence and exploitation of UNIX's considerable power as a development tool and workstation environment can begin.

See also: Mainframe and Minicomputer, MS.DOS, Operating System, OS/ 2, Personal Computer, Workstation

No one in IT is neutral about UNIX. Technical specialists tend to be enthusiastic proponents; while IS managers tend to be cautious, largely because of the as yet unclear and unproven opportunities and benefits of using UNIX in core and large-scale transaction processing systems.

User   Users are an abstraction that Information Services' professionals talk about either as the principal community they serve or the cross they bear. They are better thought of as clients and colleagues. That the worlds of IS professionals and "real" people have historically been separate, both psychologically and physically, is a major impediment to doing so. Prior to the diffusion of personal computers, users had little contact with IS staff. Technical staff, hired for their technical aptitude and qualifications and promoted on the basis of the quality of their technical work, inhabited data centers often many miles removed from business offices.

Skilled technical people, especially in the most specialized areas of IT, still tend to be "different." It is this difference, particularly the highly analytic and structured mode of thinking that allows them to handle the complex and lengthy process of large-scale software development, that makes them valuable to businesses. It became increasingly apparent in the early 1980s that many failures of new systems were attributable to lack of understanding of clients and their work and lack of meaningful involvement in the design and implementation processes. Every first-rate Information Services organization began to create new methods, groups, and services to bridge the IT-business culture divide. This has not been easy in terms of finding and building skills and developing career rewards, methods, and mutual understanding. A new style of "business analyst," possessing hybrid skills, either strong business knowledge plus adequate technical capability, or vice-versa, has emerged in many IS groups.

It is no exaggeration to say that the effectiveness of any firm's IT strategy is today determined more by organizational than by technical issues. IS leadership contributes most when it makes service and support a priority rather than a grudging necessity. Business managers contribute most when they assign skilled staff, not expendable mediocrities, to their IT activities and encourage real dialogue with the Information Systems unit.

See also: Data Center, End-User Computing

User Friendly   In the IT context, user friendly is generally understood to mean that computer software or equipment is easy-to-

Calling real people "users" is a reminder of how little attention most IT systems developers paid to people in the data processing and MIS eras. Imagine a hotel calling its guests "users."

use, incorporates a natural-seeming interface, and is flexible. The widespread use of the term notwithstanding, most people find computers hard to use. The more "functionality" a computer offers, in terms of range of options in use, modes of display, telecommunications, and peripheral devices, the more familiar the user has to be with the details of the operating system and hardware. True user friendliness means hiding details and handling all housekeeping and management functions so that users can concentrate on their work rather than on the computer. This is becoming a major problem in many businesses. Staff quickly learn to run, say, a spreadsheet program on a stand-alone personal computer. Later, they add a word processing package, a modem for accessing data and sending electronic mail, then a database management system and a laser printer. At some point the personal computer is linked to the department's local area network. By this time, however user friendly the individual elements are, the aggregation of hardware, telecommunications facilities, and software has reached a level of complexity equivalent to that of a 1970s data processing department. Such a system must be supported by technical specialists and people who understand the details of its operation. Many Information Systems groups provide "hot lines," which users can call with problems, and many business units are creating new support staff jobs.

Computers are still hard to use, but they are less user hostile than last year. Every innovation that makes the user interface more "intuitive" moves the field forward.

Some general principles have emerged for making systems user friendly. The first, and perhaps most essential, is to eliminate the need for users to type instructions to the operating system. One way to do this is to present users with a pictorial, or graphical, choice of options. The graphical user interface (GUI) made popular by Apple's Macintosh personal computer is an example of this. Microsoft's Windows provides this style of user interface for IBM and IBM-compatible personal computers. The underlying principle of GUIs is to make the use of systems "intuitive" to users.

The second principle for inceasing user friendliness is organizational. Firms standardizing on software for word processing, spreadsheets, and other widely used applications are not trying to control users or enforce uniformity, but rather to minimize problems of incompatibility between systems and make it easier to support users by enabling IS staff to move between departments without having to learn different systems.

The only people who can testify that systems are user friendly are users. That is why they must be included in the design of any system that affects their work from the begining of the project. No one can design a system for others without understanding how they work and think. The best way to do that is to make systems design a joint process and to use prototypes so that users can learn by using and developers by watching.

See also: End-User Computing, Prototyping, User Interface

User Interface   User interface refers to the dialogue between a human being and a computer system. The traditional user interface is the keyboard, from which commands are typed into a computer. The innovation of the on-screen menu, which presents a selection of commands that may be invoked at any junction in an application, has saved newer users much page turning in software manuals. An evolution of the traditional menu displays options as graphical images, termed icons. This type of graphical user interface generally includes a mouse, a device attached to the personal computer that can be moved to position a pointer or cursor, over an icon. Clicking the mouse (pressing a button on the top of it) indicates that the item is to be selected.

The interface is the system from the user's perspective.

Emerging types of user interface include tablets that may be written on with a special pen, light pens that can write directly on the computer screen, and voice commands to the computer. These are in the early stages of development; many improvements will be needed in hardware and software before they are ready for everyday use. Voice input, in which the computer recognizes spoken words, is improving rapidly and is likely to move into the mainstream of computer use during the coming decade.

See also: Bar Code, Graphical User Interface, Image Technology, MS.DOS

Value-Added Network (VAN)   A value-added network, or VAN, is a network service that provides other than POTS, "plain old telephone service" or basic transmission links. These are the regulated domain of transmission suppliers. VANs add something of value to transmission: electronic data interchange services, electronic mail, information services, and so forth. They fall between the public networks that are available to any firm and the private networks leased by single companies from telecommunications suppliers.

In the international arena, VANs offer transnational firms with many advantages. Because they provide "one-stop shopping," companies need not deal individually with each national PTT, and their long-term agreements with international communications suppliers and good working relationships with national telecommunications authorities spare users what can be a heavy burden in planning, negotiation, operations, and budgeting.

The major U.S. players in the international VAN market are also the principal competitors in the domestic long-distance telephone market. Most entered the VAN market through acquisitions. AT&T bought the British firm Istel for more than $300 million. MCI acquired a position in Infonet, the fastest-growing international VAN provider. But acquisitions work both ways, and British Telecom acquired the U.S. Tymnet. VAN providers, which see the globalization of business as a tremendous opportunity and electronic data interchange as a major driver of growth, are prepared to wire the world.

See also: *International Telecommunications, Network, Telecommunications*

VAN   See Value-Added Network

Very Small Aperture Terminal (VSAT)   Very small aperture terminals, or VSATs, are satellite earth stations that are very small, typically 5 feet or less in diameter, enabling them to be located and relocated quickly and opening up opportunities for linking many locations to which it would be impractical to run cables. As of 1991, a VSAT cost between $2,000 and $15,000 for the "dish" and about $80,000 for the master "hub," which transmits and receives data.

Firms adopting VSAT technology are finding that it opens up new ways of thinking about business and organization. Imagine, for example, opening a bank of automated teller machines at a major sporting event, using a VSAT to link the ATMs to the central processing systems, or linking an oil exploration site to scientific computers for sending and analyzing seismic data. VSATs can update price lists in a retailing chain's stores nightly, even those in rural locations, and in engineering construction can link a personal computer at a desert construction site to the head office. The Gulf War showed the importance and value of satellite communications in television reporting; CNN moved its dishes with its journalists.

VSAT is especially effective and cost-efficient for organizations that have many units — stores, branches, or offices — spread over a wide geographic area. For this reason the retailing industry has been the leader in deploying VSATs. K mart, for instance, replaced its 29 separate telecommunications networks with a VSAT network that linked its headquarters with its 2,200 stores. The network is the firm's information highway. It handles a wide range of applications including the daily transmission of all purchasing and sales information sent to K mart's central computers. Credit card authorizations that took from 3–15 minutes to process when telephone lines were jammed during the Christmas shopping period take 13 seconds with the network.

K mart senior management is using the video capabilities of the VSAT network to repersonalize management. The firm calculates that visiting each store to meet and collect feedback from its 340,000 employees would take 5 1/2 years. The network has thus become the vehicle for these "visits." K mart's 1988 financial results were announced by its chairman over the network, and store employees meet electronically with merchandisers.

K mart estimates that the VSAT network is 30 percent less expensive than leased "terrestrial" lines and that the full cost of video broadcasting is a mere 50 cents per hour per store. Downtime is just half an hour per year. K mart's figures match those of other VSAT users such as Child World and Frito-Lay.

See also: Business Television, Distributed Systems, Mobile Communication, Satellite, Videoconferencing

Videoconferencing Videoconferencing uses telecommunications to bring people at physically remote locations together for

PCs were driven by user creativity. VSAT will be, too. The retailing industry is the leader here—along with CNN in Iraq and Kuwait. K mart's cost of full-motion television quality videoconferencing (for meetings and training) its 2,200 stores is 50 cents per hour per store through VSAT.

meetings. Each location in a videoconferencing system needs a room equipped to send and receive video, generally via satellite. A typical room with video capability costs between $50,000 and $250,000. The cost of a one-hour California to New York City videoconference dropped from $750 in 1990 to just $250 in 1991. One maker of videoconferencing equipment now offers a complete system for less than $40,000.

Videoconferencing has been in wide use for several decades. A few companies have used it heavily throughout that time to manage projects across widely separated locations. But growth in general has been slow, partly because of cost, but more so because electronic meetings have tended to be seen as a simple substitute for travel, which is generally an inadequate justification for the capital investment required, or because people feel that they cannot substitute for face-to-face meetings. Costs are now dropping rapidly, thanks largely to "codec" equipment that compresses the expensive transmission signal needed for television-quality conferencing. And in an era of VHS home cameras and video, most people are fully at ease, often to their surprise, when "on camera."

Videoconferencing helps organizations handle time, complexity, and distance, repersonalize leadership by enabling senior managers to meet more regularly with staff, and manage project and management review meetings and crises. Some examples of the value of videoconferencing were reported in the *New York Times* in early 1991. One manager described Air Products and Chemicals' use of videoconferencing to link its Pennsylvania office to the Houston offices of Bechtel, with which it was working on a joint venture: "In some cases, we've cut weeks out of the whole construction process," the manager explained; "we can get key people in two locations to sit down together, work through their problems and issues, and then go off and implement the changes without ever having been in the same room."

Videoconferencing is not a substitute for travel, any more than the telephone is.

Organizations that provide videoconferencing facilities that can be booked by the hour, often on one-day's notice, span most major international cities. The cost is generally about the same as first-class airfare for one person.

Air travel is becoming more stressful, expensive, and inconvenient at the same time that business is becoming more dependent on teams working across functions, locations, countries, and even companies, and time-based competition and coordination are more of a priority. The experiences of the many firms that use videoconferencing for project and crisis management problem-solving, education, personalizing management, streamlining the bureaucracy, and eliminating delays that impede rapid coordination and decision making strongly demonstrate that business managers should examine it as a major opportunity to gain organizational advantage that can translate into competitive advantage.

See also: Business Television, Electronic Mail

Videotex   Videotex is a generic term for two-way interactive services delivered to users via personal computers or specially provided simple workstations. Videotex originated in Europe. It was expected to bring shopping, banking, newspapers, and masses of information directly into the home. With few exceptions, one of them France Telecom's famous Minitel, it has been a bust. Minitel created a market by providing free to telephone subscribers terminals that were initially used for directory inquiries. Other information providers quickly added services, ranging from product information to sex clubs. Despite its widespread use, Minitel loses a great deal of money, an estimated $800 million in 1990.

U.S efforts to create consumer videotex services have consistently failed, with large losses. Knight-Ridder, the newspaper chain, was able to enroll only 20,000 subscribers to its videotex service and wrote off more than $50 million. The Trintex consortium established by Sears, IBM, and CBS, lost at least $300 million on its videotex venture, and NYNEX, the Regional Bell Operating Company, in 1991 abandoned its Info-Look Gateway Services, a collection of about 200 pay-as-you-go information services ranging from electronic bulletin boards to games to home shopping, which had managed to attract only 12,500 subscribers, fewer than 2,000 of whom used it regularly. The Prodigy service, the latest effort in this area, though it has yet to reach a break-even level of subscribers, has managed to gradually increase the number of its users over the past three years. Prodigy is a well-funded partnership of Sears and IBM that provides a wide range of services for a basic fee of $13 per month. The services include electronic mail, educational games, on-line encyclopedias, travel services (including direct use of American Airlines' EAASY Sabre reservation system), numerous shopping opportunities (with home delivery), film synopses and reviews, and business and financial services information, including discount security trading. The service can be accessed from any standard IBM, IBM-compatible, or Macintosh personal computer over a standard telephone line.

The only consumer-focused videotex service that has been successful is France Telecom's legendary Minitel. Given that it lost an estimated $800 million in 1990, even that "success" is questionable. Prodigy is the latest effort to turn personal computers into profits via videotex.

It is too early to tell if Prodigy will be the breakthrough product that turns electronic consumer services into a real money maker. System operation is slow and early versions were clumsy, but huge amounts of money have been spent on special offers and promotions. Perhaps this time...

The principal problems with videotex have been cumbersome and slow communications and lack of consumer interest in the services being offered. Suppliers have yet to find the single self-justifying, immediate benefit application. Nintendo is taking a shot at finding it; the company is developing an electronic telecommunications capability to link its game control units to a network. Perhaps Game Boy will ignite the spark that sets the consumer electronic services market ablaze.

See also: *Smart Card, Value-Added Network*

Virus   A virus is a software program that is intended to take over a computer's operation. Viruses are generally infiltrated into computers by "hackers" who understand some detail of the operating system that enables them to attach the virus to another program. At some point, often on a special date such as Christmas or April Fool's Day, the virus reveals itself, taking over and erasing files or multiplying itself and filling a computer or even a network of computers. Some viruses are harmless and merely display humorous messages, but others can create, as their name implies, a plague.

Hackers are individuals whose lives center around doing clever things with computers. Most are not computer criminals and few become involved in trying to introduce viruses into computers. But one way hackers can show off to their peers is by infiltrating supposedly secure systems. One of the best-known viruses was the work of a Cornell student who had no intention of doing damage, though his virus brought down university computers across the United States.

Viruses are a very real threat to companies. The damage they can do is literally incalculable. Many companies insist that no software not bought directly from the company that developed it can be installed on their computers. Special-purpose software programs are available that check for well-known viruses.

See also: Security

Voice Recognition   Voice recognition refers to the ability of a computer to interpret spoken words. There are many applications in which the most efficient and simple way to communicate with computers would be through speech. Air traffic controllers, bank tellers, and manufacturing production staff could use voice recognition capability to issue instructions to a computer naturally and quickly, leaving their hands free to operate other devices.

There are two aspects of voice recognition, understanding the word and understanding what it means. There has been rapid progress in the past few years in developing systems that can reliably recognize a limited vocabulary, distinguishing "one" from "three" and "nine," for example. These systems can handle variations in voice pitch and even accent. They operate by comparing the speech input signal with stored patterns for given words and estimating the probability of match with each. This requires very large and very fast chips that can process the signals at least as fast as a person speaks.

Far more difficult is understanding the meaning of what is said. Consider the following sentence: "I want you right now to write a letter to Mr. Wright." A prototype system developed by IBM can in fact correctly input and display this sentence, spelled correctly, on its screen. Because the system requires massive computing power, it will be several years before systems like it are widely available to enable people to dictate memos to computers. But once a system works in the

A system at IBM's telecommunications research laboratory in France can correctly convert the following spoken message to a written display on the screen: "I want you right now to write a letter to Mr. Wright." Voice recognition will certainly be a growth area of the late 1990s.

laboratory, however expensive it might be, it is almost certain to exploit the 20–30 percent annual improvement in the cost and power of computer hardware and rapidly move first to a limited system in terms of functionality and then to mass production.

VSAT See Very Small Aperture Terminal

WAN See Wide Area Network

Wide Area Network A wide area network, or WAN, involves complex transmission facilities that link widely separated locations. In the early 1980s, high-speed transmission was pretty much limited to wide area networks. That has changed dramatically as fiber optics technology has driven rapid increases in the speed of local area networks. Local area networks, or LANs, have become the principal building block for many departmental uses of telecommunications, often with no forward planning for interconnecting separate LANs or linking them to wide area networks. LANs and WANs are based on fundamentally different technical bases.

The technology of wide area networks is very different from that of local area networks. Interconnecting the two ranges from a challenge to a disaster in most companies.

The primary criteria for choosing a wide area network in the United States are cost and reliability. All major providers of private and public network services offer a wide range of high-speed facilities at aggressively competitive prices. Firms have four main options: (1) use the public network operated by AT&T, which offers the most flexibility in terms of planning, since companies pay only for what they use and have access to a giant, nationwide resource; (2) contract with a transmission provider for a private, leased line network that guarantees the firm a fixed level of capacity at a fixed price; (3) contract for a virtual private network, a technically sophisticated variant of a private network, that provides greater flexibility in pricing and requires a smaller capital investment; and (4) install a VSAT private network that employs satellite transmission to connect hundreds or thousands of small earth-station "dishes."

See also: International Telecommunications, Local Area Network, Network, Telecommunications, Transmission

The explosive success of Microsoft Windows shows how important ease of use and graphical point-and-go interfaces are to users of personal computers.

Windows   In 1990, Microsoft, the company that created the MS.DOS operating system that became the basis for IBM and IBM-compatible personal computers and worked closely with IBM on the development the OS/2 operating system for the PS/2 series of personal computers, launched a new version of its Windows product that turned an MS.DOS machine into an Apple Macintosh look-alike. Early versions of Windows were clumsy and slow. The new product was an instant success, selling two million copies in its first year, though it continues to be criticized for being slow, requiring a powerful personal computer to run efficiently, and for being less easy to use than a Mac.

Many businesses, perceiving it to provide all the advantages of MS.DOS personal computers and Macs have adopted Windows enthusiastically. They welcome the Mac style of graphical presentation, which is generally seen as more intuitive to learn and use, and shed no tears for the complex and user-hostile MS.DOS commands and mode of interaction between user and system that it replaces.

As of 1991, there are many uncertainties about the progress of MS.DOS and Windows versus OS/2, which was expected to rapidly replace DOS. It may be two years before the trend becomes clear.

See also: Graphical User Interface, Operating System, User Interface

Word processing has not created the paperless office as many experts predicted it would.

Word Processing   Ten years ago, word processing was a major innovation. Today, it is commonplace. Then, word processors required specialized equipment. Now, word processing software packages are routinely run on personal computers. Word processing is by far the primary use of personal computers, with spreadsheet software second.

See also: Software

Workstation   A personal computer or terminal that operates fairly continuously as part of a networked system is often called a workstation. But the term is also used more restrictively to refer to powerful, specialized microcomputers of the type used in engineering and design applications. Computer-aided engineering and computer-aided design workstations are capable of rapid simulation and calculation and have very high-resolution screens that can display, refresh, and rotate images of photographic quality in full color.

See also: Personal Computer, Terminal

WYSIWYG   Wysiwyg (pronounced wizzywig) stands for "what you see is what you get." It means that when you use a word processing or graphics software package the reports and images shown on the screen will be printed exactly as they appear. That may seem like no big deal, but many early software systems displayed the "control" characters used to indicate such features as underlining, new paragraph, or italics. WISIWYG is now well established as a general principle for designing software.

See also: Jargon and Acronyms, User Interface

X12   X12 is the principal ANSI standard for electronic data interchange. It is a technical standard that is the basis for several business standards that define how firms can send transaction documents to and from one another's computers without having to adopt the same form layouts.

See also: ANSI, Electronic Data Interchange, Standards

X.25   The basis of the X.25 standard is packet-switching, a data transmission technique suited to high-volume "bursty" telecommunications traffic (i.e., abundant short messages typical of electronic mail, electronic data interchange, and electronic funds transfers). Packet-switching incurs substantial overhead that introduces delay in transmissions, a shortcoming being overcome by recent developments in "fast packet-switching." One breakthrough, termed "frame relay," speeds packets through an X.25 network ten times faster.

The security limitations inherent in most X.25 networks are less a function of the standard than of the public data networks that employ it, their function being to facilitate, not constrain, access.

Inasmuch as it is the basis for so many international public data and value-added networks, X.25 is an essential part of the information

Workstations offer technical performance that often exceeds that of the largest mainframe machines of just five years ago, at a fraction of the cost. But they are costly in comparison with personal computers—typically five to ten times as much.

Not to adopt electronic data interchange by the mid-1990s will be as dumb as not using telephones today. X12 is one of the central standards for EDI implementation.

architecture of firm that must operate across borders. Yet performance and efficiency increasingly favor alternative schemes.

See also: International Telecommunications, Packet-Switching, Standards

X.400 may be the most important telecommunications standard of the last ten years; it opens up a new world of linked electronic mail services, and low-cost electronic data interchange opportunities.

X.400   X.400 defines the electronic equivalent of envelopes for voice mail, telex, fax, and electronic mail messages, and is independent of the type of telecommunications transmission and receiving device. It opens up a whole new range of business opportunities related to low-cost electronic data interchange and organization-wide use of electronic mail. Many standards, though important from a technical perspective, are not directly relevant to business planning. But major standards that addresses interfirm links for exchanging business information, as X.400 does, should be part of the vocabulary of business managers.

See also: Electonic Data Interchange, Standards

Index

ABOUT THE AUTHOR

Peter G.W. Keen is the executive director of the International Center for Information Technologies. A graduate of Oxford University and the Harvard Business School, he has served on the faculties of the Harvard Business School, MIT's Sloan School of Management, the London Business School, and the Stanford Business School and is currently a visiting professor at Fordham University. Keen is the author of *Competing in Time: Using Telecommunications for Competitive Advantage* (Ballinger, 1986) and *Shaping the Future: Business Design through Information Technology* (Harvard Business School Press, 1991) and co-author of *Decision Support Systems: An Organizational Perspective* (Addison-Wesley, 1978).